Your Living Family Tree

Discover Your Family Stories

Your Living Family Tree

Discover Your Family Stories

The Easy, Step-by-step Guide

Capture the Moment
Ask the Right Questions
Inspire Future Generations

Mary-Jill Bellhouse

BALBOA
PRESS

A DIVISION OF HAY HOUSE

Illustrations copyright © Jess Racklyeft, 2013.
Cover Artwork copyright © Jennifer Lommers, 2010.

Balboa Press books may be ordered through booksellers or by contacting:

Balboa Press
A Division of Hay House
1663 Liberty Drive
Bloomington, IN 47403
www.balboapress.com.au
1 (877) 407-4847

Because of the dynamic nature of the Internet, any web addresses or links contained in this book may have changed since publication and may no longer be valid. The views expressed in this work are solely those of the author and do not necessarily reflect the views of the publisher, and the publisher hereby disclaims any responsibility for them.

This publication is designed to provide competent and reliable information regarding the subject matters covered. However, it is sold with the understanding that the author and publisher are not engaged in rendering legal, financial, or other professional advice. Laws and practices often vary from country to country and from state to state, and if legal or other expert assistance is required, the services of a professional should be sought. The author and publisher specifically disclaim any liability that is incurred from the use or application of the contents of this book.

This product is supplied "as is" and without warranties. All warranties, express or implied, are hereby disclaimed. The author and publisher make no representation or warranties of any kind with regard to the accuracy or completeness of the contents of this book. Use of this product constitutes acceptance of the "No Liability" policy. If you do not agree with this policy, you are not permitted to use this product.

Any extracts used in this book are directly from publicly accessible file archives and are used for "air use" purposes only to illustrate various points made.

Any people depicted in stock imagery provided by Thinkstock are models, and such images are being used for illustrative purposes only. Certain stock imagery © Thinkstock.

Printed in the United States of America.

ISBN: 978-1-4525-2477-1 (sc)

Balboa Press rev. date: 09/04/2014

Dedication Page

For Rachel, Todd, Bella, and Chantel, with Joey and Kent.
For believing in me.

Contents

List of Illustrations

Acknowledgements

Enormous thanks to my children, Rachel, Todd, Bella, and Chantel, together with Joey and Kent, and to Lynn, Di, and Fi for believing in me and encouraging me to keep going. I am so lucky to have you all on my side.

Thank you to Hay House for introducing me to Balboa Press at their 2012 Writers' Workshop in Sydney. You gave me the confidence to believe I can actually live my dream and become an author.

Thanks to Oral History Australia for their dedication to teaching the practice of oral history through their website, workshops, and conferences.

Finally, thanks also to Dulcie Holland and Alan Bellhouse, my late aunt and uncle; your interviews with the National Library of Australia Oral History Program illuminated my path.

Introduction

Who were your ancestors? Your family tree might tell you their names, where they lived, and what they did for a living, but wouldn't you like to know more? What were they were really like? Did you inherit any of their looks or personality traits? What kinds of experiences did they have, and who were the people who shaped their lives?

We can't ask those who have already gone, but what if future generations of your family could discover the answers to these questions, and more, by listening to their ancestors telling their stories?

You can record conversations with your living relatives about their own unique life experiences and about your family history. When the fascinating patchwork of stories is stitched together, a living branch, with living ancestors, appears on your family tree.

A familiar conversational setting is an ideal environment in which to record relaxed interviews. Family members might also reveal details about their lives that they would not normally consider sharing and who knows, they may even reveal the answers to some family secrets or unleash a skeleton from the family closet!

Twenty years ago, I discovered that my aunt and uncle had been interviewed by the National Library of Australia Oral History Program. When I listened to the recordings I heard family stories being told that I'd never heard before, and I learnt lots of interesting information about my ancestors. I thought, *Wouldn't it be wonderful if other people could listen to their family's history being told, and wouldn't it be even better if they could hear it from their* living *relatives?* So I learnt how to conduct personal interviews—what equipment to use, what questions to ask, and the best way to ask them—and for the past twenty years I have been professionally recording family and community oral histories.

However, along the way people said to me, "I'd love to record my own family history, but I don't know where to begin." So I created this easy, step-by-step guide to give you a basic understanding of what you need to know to get started on recording conversations with your relatives about your own family history. It's an entry-level text, written with the assumption that you, the reader, are a novice interviewer, but if you've got experience in this field already, so much the better. There's no complex jargon, and you don't have to spend frustrating hours searching the Internet for instructions on how to interview or what questions to ask. I've drawn upon my years of experience as a family history interviewer to provide you with tips on just about everything you'll need to know to get the most out of your interview. Some of these tips are repeated throughout the book because they are relevant to more than one section, but you don't have to follow them to the letter. They are simply offered to give you confidence as you commence, and then progress, with your interviews. Don't be too concerned about "doing it right." It won't take long for you to develop your own process. Just keep an open mind, stay calm, and do the best you can.

Before you start, it's a good idea to think about what you'd like to know about your family and who would be the best person to ask first (we'll call him or her your "interviewee"). Then you can decide which questions to ask using the list in chapter 7 as a guide. Questions designed to elicit candid, relaxed responses from your interviewee are grouped into logical, chronological sections: your early family years and relatives; your childhood family home; family life when you were growing up; primary and high school years; further education; your adult life and career; love and marriage; your first home after marriage; starting a family; the war years; religion; travel and other interests; and looking back and taking stock. When the fascinating patchwork of answers is stitched together, a living branch will appear on your family tree.

Your family memories can be preserved by using a variety of media that captures in real time people's feelings, expressions, and nuances of language, but for the purposes of this book and to give you the full benefit of my own experience, I have concentrated on the practice of audio recording.

By way of wider background, the recording of a person's story in his or her own words is also known as "oral history." Many oral histories have preserved the memories and unique life experiences of people who have become rich and famous, or have been involved in historical events, or excelled in a particular field, but history often fails to include the everyday memories and experiences of people from ordinary walks of life. They too have interesting experiences and wisdom of historical importance to share.

A family tree provides valuable genealogical information based on detailed research of available written records, but oral histories can help us to understand society's changing values and attitudes and the events that have shaped it into what it is today. Live recordings of our own family history can also provide a link to connect and inspire current and future generations. We develop a unique familial connection with our ancestors when we listen to our family members—each with his or her own different memories and perspectives—describing the people and experiences that shaped their lives and telling the stories behind family anecdotes, photos, letters, heirlooms, and other family memorabilia. Their struggles and achievements can inspire and help us to gain a clearer insight into the events in our own lives and even to understand more about our purpose in life.

In the past, when generations of families shared the same house or lived close by, the elders passed on the family history by word of mouth in the form of stories, experiences, traditions, beliefs, and wisdom. However, in today's rapidly changing and increasingly mobile society, families are often geographically separated by work and other commitments. They don't always have the opportunity or the time to sit down and talk with the older folks about their recollections of the past; unless someone records these stories before they pass on, their precious memories are lost forever.

Did you know that you could be the link for up to five generations of the branches on your family tree? Your great-grandparents, grandparents, parents, children, and grandchildren, as well as your brothers, sisters, aunts, uncles, and even family friends, all have stories to share about their lives and about your family's history. So it is very important that you continue to collect and add as many stories as you can to create and perpetuate the "living" branches on your family tree for future generations of your family to enjoy.

The purpose of recording your family history is usually to share the recorded information with other family members, and some people may also wish to later share it in the wider public domain (for example, write a book or set up a family history website). Regardless of what you intend to do with the recordings (including any photographs associated with the interviews), you must gain explicit permission from your interviewee to record the interview and, if applicable, to make it available for access and use by others. You should therefore always ensure that your interviewee signs a general release form that clearly states his or her permission to use the recordings, and ensure that the form also states any conditions that the interviewee wishes to place upon that permission. A sample release form that you can adapt to your own requirements, is included at the end of this book.

If you don't have the time to interview your relatives, or if a planned interview seems as if it might be too daunting for them, turn on a recorder at family gatherings to catch an informal exchange of stories, or encourage your family to record or write their own histories using the questions in this book as a guide. A friend of mine gave a copy of this book to his father, who had suffered a stroke, and slowly, as his condition improved, his father was able to write down answers to many of the questions listed in this book. This simple task improved his self-confidence, and I like to think it also contributed towards his recovery. People of all ages can apply the techniques included here, so why not ask someone in your family to record your own life history? You could also keep an audio journal using the questions in this book as a guide.

Each of us is the custodian of our own family history and by recording our family stories we can inspire future generations to feel the same. So now is the time to get started and create a living branch on your family tree. Don't wait until it's too late. Ask your relatives to tell you the stories they know about your ancestors, and at the same time ask them to share their own unique life experiences too. And as you begin this fascinating journey to discover and preserve your heritage, have fun with it, and create a lasting gift of memories for future generations to treasure.

Chapter 1

Equipment

There are many different types of portable audio recorders on the market, and updated digital technology is emerging on an almost daily basis. When you decide to record your family's history, it is important to choose equipment that provides a good-quality recording and that is affordable, reliable, and comfortable for you to use. When you choose your recording equipment, you should practice using it before you begin your interviews and then listen critically to these practice recordings to hear how you might improve them.

The oral history websites on the Internet are valuable resources for advice about the latest equipment and how to use it, and Oral History NSW is one of the best. Your nearest computer retailer, your local library, or even your local community radio station may also be able to provide helpful advice. Some oral history associations may hold short courses that include demonstrations of different kinds of recording equipment, and those in your local area may even assist with outsourcing the loan or hire of a recorder.

The basic analogue cassette recorder that uses standard or micro audio cassettes has long been replaced by digital technology. However, those old recorders were good workhorses, and many of them are still in existence, so I think they still warrant a mention here.

Whilst it is now preferable to use a high-quality digital recorder, some people may not feel entirely confident about learning how to use one or may not be in a position to outlay the cost of purchasing new equipment. However, they may have a trusty, old, analogue tape recorder, still in perfect working order, stashed away in a cupboard somewhere at home. If this is you, rather than doing nothing at all, I'd encourage you to get that old recorder out right now and start preserving your family stories. Then make sure that the completed recordings are immediately transferred to a digital format. Blank cassette tapes for analogue recorders are still available in Australia at large supermarkets, newsagents, and at specialty electrical or music retailers, so they may still be available at similar kinds of stores in other countries.

If you choose to use an analogue recorder, it is important that you follow a few basic rules to achieve a recording of the highest possible standard.

Using an Analogue Recorder

If your recorder has a power cord, use this rather than relying on batteries, which may suddenly fail. If you decide to use battery power alone, keep a supply of fresh batteries on hand; remove batteries from recording equipment after each interview and insert fresh ones before your next interview. You'll also need to purchase a set of headphones that are compatible with your equipment so that you can monitor the recording levels during the interview.

Use quality-brand sixty-minute cassette tapes (thirty minutes each side). If these aren't available, use tapes of the best quality you can find.

Purchase and use two external microphones or lapel microphones (one for you and one for your interviewee) that are compatible with your equipment. If appropriate, insert a new battery into each microphone before recording and keep spare batteries on hand.

Make sure that each side of every cassette you plan to use is clearly labelled before you start recording. Then double-check the labelling on each recorded cassette after each recording session.

At the interview, keep an eye on the time or set a digital timer and pause the recording at an appropriate place whilst you turn the tape over or insert a fresh one. It can be a bit daunting at first to ask questions, listen to your interviewee's response, watch the time, and decide the most appropriate place to pause the recording. So you could agree with your interviewee beforehand that when the tape is nearing the end of the side you are recording, you will simply raise your hand as a signal for them to finish the sentence. However, you don't have to wait until the tape has nearly ended before pausing the recording. If, for example, you're using a sixty-minute tape (thirty minutes each side), indicate to your interviewee at, say, the twenty- or twenty-five-minute mark, that you are reaching a point where you need to pause the recording. This should leave them plenty of time to finish the sentence before you actually stop the recording. It doesn't matter if you don't use the whole side of each tape in actual interview time because the recordings can be spliced together when transferred to a digital format later.

By the same token, don't worry if you get so caught up in your interviewee's story that you forget to pause the recording and the tape runs its course, cutting them off mid-sentence. Don't get flustered. Just ask your interviewee to "hold that thought," and at the beginning of the next side (or at the start of a new cassette), simply backtrack a little in your questioning and confirm what they were saying previously. This way you will maintain continuity of the conversation and keep the interviewee's train of thought flowing smoothly. When the recording is transferred to a digital format, you can, if you wish, edit the ending of the previous side by deleting the interrupted sentence; however, sometimes a recording that is not quite perfect can add to the personal authenticity of the interview. It's a bit of a juggling act to begin with, but after the first interview you'll discover what works best for you.

After each interview session, break the lugs off the cassettes so that the recordings cannot be erased or recorded over. If you can still purchase the special cassettes for this, de-magnitize your cassette recorder heads after every ten hours recording.

Store your original recorded cassettes vertically in a cool place to prevent the tapes from stretching over time and to protect them from unforeseen damage.

If at all possible, use a backup recorder during your interviews in case the original recordings are somehow lost or damaged. I use my iPhone and delete the files when I have completed the project I'm working on. It is discreet, and you can just set and forget it and then concentrate on the interview. Whilst not necessarily of archival quality, the iPhone provides a clear recording that translates into peace of mind should anything happen to your original.

Immediately after each interview, make another backup copy of the original recording. When you have completed all your interviews, transfer the backup recordings to a more stable digital format. This part of the process is as important as getting the interview itself; if you are unable to do this, you could ask your local library or a tech-savvy friend to help, or you could check out YouTube on the Internet or Google your nearest oral history association for assistance. Also, your local community radio station has the latest technical equipment and will often be willing to transfer your recordings to a digital format for a small fee.

You should also provide your interviewee with copies of the recordings in a generally accessible format, such as CD, and always use discs of the best quality you can afford. I present my clients with their CDs in a beautifully wrapped package together with a note of thanks.

Using a Digital Recorder

If you choose to invest in one of the latest digital recording devices, choose a recorder with a power cable rather than relying on batteries, which may suddenly fail; if you decide to use battery power alone, keep a supply of fresh batteries on hand. You'll also need to purchase a set of headphones that are compatible with your equipment so that you can monitor the recording levels during the interview.

I currently use a small, portable, Zoom H4N recorder that provides capacity for two independent external microphones (one for each person). It also has excellent inbuilt microphones that, on odd occasions in my experience, have proved perfectly adequate on their own. For best results, purchase and use two compatible external, condenser-type microphones that can be plugged into the recorder you are using.

If at all possible, use a backup recorder during your interviews in case the original recordings are somehow lost or damaged. I use my iPhone and delete the files when I have completed the project I'm working on. It is discreet, and you can just set and forget it and then concentrate on the interview (but remember to first turn your phone onto silent mode). Whilst not necessarily of archival quality, the iPhone provides a clear recording that translates into peace of mind should anything happen to your original.

During the interview you will need to glance at the recorder to monitor the recording levels, so you will need a flexible tripod stand for your recorder to hold it securely at an angle that will allow you to easily view the screen even when you have microphone cables attached to the base. Tripod microphone stands are also preferable. If you can, it's best to use the tall type of stand that you can place on the floor alongside yourself and your interviewee, rather than smaller ones that sit on the table, as the recorder will pick up any sound of your interviewee fidgeting with the equipment during recording. I purchased my recorder and microphone tripods from a camera store, but they may also be available at computer or music retailers.

Record your interviews in an uncompressed 24-bit/48-kHz WAV format, the level recommended for archival-quality recordings. I use an 8-GB secure digital (SD) memory card, also recommended for recording at archival-quality standard. This will give you 440 minutes of recording time on one card, but check your recorder's instructions regarding options for maximum file size.

When you've finished recording, transfer the sound files from the card to a clearly labeled file on your computer using a card reader or the USB ports in your recorder and computer. Always keep at least one copy of the original, unedited recordings in the 24/48 uncompressed WAV format either on your computer, or on an external hard drive, or on both, for safekeeping. I also store an extra copy on Dropbox, which provides an option to share your folders. CDs are no longer considered a viable alternative for archival storage, but they are still very useful for providing your interviewee with copies of the completed interviews.

Again, if you need help in transferring your sound files, ask your local library or a tech-savvy friend to help, or you could check out YouTube or Google your nearest oral history association for assistance. Also, your local community radio station has the latest technical equipment and will often, for a small fee, be willing to show you how to transfer your recordings and make copies, or they might do it for you.

Before transferring your recordings to their final playback format, you might like to edit out any unpredictable background noise interference or speech idiosyncrasies such as multiple "ums" or loud coughs. You can also reduce very long passages of silence (although it's best to leave these in). I use Audacity, which is a specialized editing software application, but if pressed for time I sometimes also outsource the transfer of sound files to CD to my local community radio station. For a small fee they will produce a clean recording (sometimes including basic speech editing) without losing any authenticity of the original recording.

As previously mentioned, you should also provide your interviewee with copies of the recordings in a generally accessible format, such as CD, and always use discs of the best quality you can afford. Again, I present my clients with a beautifully wrapped package of their recorded CDs together with a note of thanks.

Chapter 2

Before the Interview

About a week before you begin your first recording session, arrange a brief, preliminary meeting with your interviewee, in person or by telephone. Tell them about yourself and why you are interested in the family history. Confirm that they agree to the interviews being recorded and let them know how you are going to conduct them. This is your chance to put your interviewee at ease by talking in terms of having a "chat about the past" or "telling me the story of your life" rather than an "interview," which can sound a little frightening.

At the first session, request permission to take a photograph of your interviewee. Explain that this photograph will be included with the recordings or transcript.

Discuss where the interview material will be stored and what other materials you intend to produce from the recordings, such as a transcript or a book, and whether it will be uploaded to a website. Confirm that you will provide your interviewee with a copy of the recordings and any other materials produced from those recordings.

If the preliminary meeting is in person, show your interviewee a blank copy of the release form and explain its purpose. If the preliminary meeting is conducted by phone, confirm that you will mail a copy of this form to your interviewee. Explain that you will ask them to sign the form at the first interview. This gives them time to think about whether to place any restrictions on the use of the completed recordings.

Setup and Location

Discuss with your interviewee, where the interviews will take place. Let your interviewee know that the recordings can be done in the comfort of their own home or any other place in which they feel comfortable and relaxed. Explain that you will get the best recording if the interview space is made as quiet as possible. If you can, choose a quiet room with carpet on the floor—not the kitchen or a room with tiled floors as the sound tends to reverberate in these kinds of spaces. Arrange for ticking clocks and pets to be removed from the room before the interview, and make sure that there are no humming fridges or computers nearby to interfere with the quality of the recording.

Ask your interviewee not to schedule personal appointments close to the time of the interviews and ask them to be available for several hours on each day of recording. This way the interviews can be conducted in a leisurely manner, and interruptions are minimized. Also ask the interviewee not to schedule cleaners and gardeners to work on the days you will be interviewing. I know from personal experience that lawnmowers, hedge cutters, and vacuum cleaners are not ideal background noise in a recording!

Despite all your careful planning, interruptions and noises beyond your control will inevitably occur. So don't worry unduly if, during the interview, a dog barks, a bird chirps outside the window, or a car goes by, as these occasional sounds of life can often add texture to the recording.

Prepare Your Subject

Reassure your interviewee that, unless they specifically request differently, it will be just the two of you involved in the interview process.

On the one hand, I find it preferable not to interview two or more people at the same time because each person, by virtue of their different life experiences, holds different perceptions of events. In an interview involving two or more people, either quite heated discussions can occur when each person believes that his or her memory of an event is correct, or the interview simply becomes a conversation between the interviewees and the interview structure is lost. I also find that it's not a good idea for other family members to be present when you are interviewing a person about his or her life experiences, as the interviewee may not feel comfortable about opening up or may be reluctant to give a candid response to your questions; here again, the family members may be tempted to correct the interviewee with their own perceptions or memories of the events being discussed.

On the other hand, interviews between two or more people can be interesting because each interviewee may reinforce the other by remembering the same events from a different perspective, one having had a positive experience of the event and the other a negative one.

So you will need to assess for yourself the merits of including another person in your interviews. If you do decide to interview two people at the same time, place the microphone between them and sit them close together so that both their voices are clearly heard in the recording.

Gather as much information about your interviewee as possible to help you to decide which questions to ask. Ask your interviewee to complete a brief pre-interview form that will provide you with details of names, dates, and places. This form will provide an easy ice-breaker and will allow your interviewee to relax as you go over these details at the start of your first recording session. A sample form that you can adapt to your own requirements is included at the end of this book.

Provide your interviewee with a list of the questions you intend to ask, or an overview of the topics you'd like to cover. This can give them time to recall people and events that they may not have thought about in a long time. Let the interviewee know that answers do not need to be prepared in advance, and reiterate that the purpose of the interview is for them to tell their story in their own way. At this point your interviewee may want to begin telling you some of their stories; gently discourage this by saying that you are looking forward to hearing all the details in the recorded interview.

Reassure your interviewee that they do not have to answer certain questions if they don't feel comfortable doing so, and give them the opportunity at the outset to let you know if there are any topics that they do not want to discuss. Don't surprise your interviewee by suddenly asking potentially sensitive questions at the interview.

Explain to your interviewee that it is their story and that you will not be making any comments of your own during the interview, as this may detract from the authenticity of the recording. Explain that you will express your interest in what they are saying by leaning forward, maintaining eye contact, nodding, smiling, and, if appropriate, "laughing silently." This takes a bit of practice, but is well worth the effort to get a good recording.

Schedule a time in advance for each interview and re-confirm with the interviewee the day beforehand.

Familiarize yourself thoroughly with your equipment before the first interview.

Before You Leave Home for Each Interview

Set up and test your recording equipment. If required, insert fresh batteries into your recording device and microphones.

Record a brief sound check, and also check through your headphones that the recording is clear. (Later, you can record your formal interview introduction over this as a final sound check.)

Ensure you have packed the items on your checklist (below).

Clearly identify the interview details onto whatever medium you are using to record.

If you are using **analogue** cassettes, label in pencil each side of, say, two or three cassettes for a one-hour interview. You will probably only use one, but it's good to have a few extra cassettes already labelled just in case you need them. After the final interview, print new labels or re-write the existing ones in ink and attach them to the cassettes.

If you are recording in a **digital** format, clearly identify your files on your recorder or on your computer.

Labelling or identification should include

- the name of the interviewee;
- your name as interviewer;
- the date and place of the interview; and
- the position of the recording in the interview sequence (for example, the first recording of three is written as *1/3*).

Checklist of equipment to take to each interview (as required):

- Audio recorder, including power cord and recorder stand
- Spare batteries
- Spare SD or other digital card
- External microphones, cables, and stands
- Headphones for monitoring your recording
- Extension cord, power board, and double adapter
- List of prepared questions and release form
- Completed pre-interview form, clipboard, pen, and paper
- Watch or timer
- Backup recorder or iPhone
- Camera
- Extra cassettes if using an analogue recorder

Chapter 3

At the Interview

Be punctual. You want your interviewee to be relaxed when you arrive, not anxiously wondering if you have forgotten the appointment.

When you have settled, do another sound check to make sure your equipment is working properly. Explain to your interviewee that you will be wearing headphones to monitor the recording levels throughout the interview. This might look very formal so if you find that it is intimidating or distracting to your interviewee, then discreetly pop your headphones on at regular intervals throughout the interview to check that the recording is clear.

Ensure that any bags or equipment not being used during the interview are stowed out of sight so that the area around you is kept tidy and free of distractions.

Make sure that equipment leads and extension cords are secured firmly out of the way, as they can become a safety hazard if tripped over.

It can be quite an overwhelming process to be the subject of an interview, and during a recording session interviewees tend to unconsciously fidget with whatever is in front of them. Therefore, keep the area directly in front of your interviewee clear so distractions that may spoil the recording are minimized. Having said that, you can't predict what might cause a distraction, and often the best-laid plans go awry. I interviewed a very sprightly ninety-eight-year-old man who continually swept his hand back and forth across the tablecloth in front of him to emphasize certain points in the conversation. Whilst the gesture itself was not too noisy, the "swishing" sound was very loud when picked up by the recorder. Eventually I paused the interview and politely asked the gentleman if he would mind keeping his hands still. I explained that the recorder was extremely sensitive and that it was picking up the sound of his hand on the tablecloth, so he was more than happy to keep his hands in his lap for the remainder of the interview!

Anchor your microphones onto tall stands that you can place on the floor alongside yourself and your interviewee to minimize distractions such as those mentioned above. If you wish to use smaller microphone stands that sit on the table, position them on a solid surface, ideally at approximately a hand-span from the interviewee's mouth. Whether you're using stand-alone or lapel microphones, explain to your interviewee that the microphone is very sensitive and shouldn't be touched during the interview.

During your recording session, it is best to sit at a slight angle to your interviewee, as this will allow eye contact without the interviewee feeling intimidated.

Check once more that the room is free of extraneous noise and distractions and ask other people in the household to respect your privacy for the duration of the interview. As mentioned previously, despite all your careful planning, interruptions and noises that are beyond your control will occur during the interview. Sometimes it adds to the fabric of the interview to hear natural sounds of the interviewee's personal environment, so don't worry if a dog barks or a bird chirps outside the window. If the phone rings and needs to be answered, pause the recording until your interviewee is ready to continue. I once interviewed an elderly gentleman whose next-door neighbour decided to mow his lawn and then used an electric hedge trimmer whilst we were recording. When we realised that the noise was going to continue for some time, we had no choice but to pause the recording and have a cup of tea until he had finished; I was later able to edit down some of the background noise we hadn't caught earlier, and the final recording survived fairly well intact.

With permission, take a photograph of your interviewee. This can be copied to a CD or used in a transcript or other manuscript format you might produce later.

Put Your Interviewee, and Yourself, at Ease

If you plan on recording several interviews, it's a good idea to organise them a week apart and at the same time each week. Don't forget to confirm a day or two beforehand that your interviewee is still available.

Place a jug of water and glasses nearby for yourself and the interviewee, but take care to position them away from your recording equipment.

Develop a familiar routine that you follow at the beginning of each interview. What works for me is to settle the interviewee in a comfortable chair and help them to relax by chatting casually for a few minutes. Then I briefly recap how I am going to conduct the interviews before starting the recording. This whole process might be a "big thing" for your interviewee, and they may feel nervous or apprehensive, so be patient and always mindful of their feelings. Remember that if your interviewee is elderly and/ or lives on their own, you may be the first person they have spoken to all week and they may be anxious and hesitant, so don't rush them.

Reassure your interviewee that they can ask you to stop the interview at any time if a break is needed or if they are concerned about the direction of the questions.

At the start of the first interview, remind your interviewee of a story you have heard them tell in the past or that they began to tell you at your pre-interview chat. This will break the ice and will relax you both before you move to your preferred line of questioning. Start each subsequent interview with a brief recap of the topics you covered in the previous session.

As previously mentioned, during each interview you will have to concentrate on several things at once: monitoring your recording equipment, maintaining eye contact with the interviewee, following the interviewee's train of thought, keeping one step ahead with your questions, and keeping the interviewee on track. Don't worry about doing it all *correctly*; you'll fall into a comfortable rhythm after the first interview.

Keep your interviews to no more than one hour at a time; any more is tiring, especially if the interviewee is elderly. I interviewed a man who fell asleep during our first interview. He was quite ill at the time, so during subsequent interviews I closely observed his energy level and was able to gauge when he had had enough.

On the other hand, my ninety-eight-year-old gentleman, mentioned in the previous section, virtually memorized the list of topics I gave him beforehand and proceeded to tell his life story before I had a chance to ask any questions! I gently reminded him that whilst I was keen to hear his story, we needed to work within broadly pre-arranged guidelines, as his interview was part of an external project. So he agreed to let me direct the interview, but I had to keep my wits about me, as he tried to take the reins whenever he could!

As you progress with your interviews, you will learn to recognize the opportunities that allow you to guide your interviewee's story down an interesting path, sometimes off on a tangent away from the question you were originally exploring. However, you must also learn to recognize the point at which you should guide your interviewee back into the relevant structure of the interview. In other words, explore any interesting stories that come up, even if they seem to be unrelated to the question you have just asked. Then, when you think the time is right, gently guide the interview back on track. You will find that it really is quite easy to do this, and you can discover along the way some fascinating answers to questions you might never have thought to ask!

Chapter 4

After the Interview

At the end of each interview, be sure to thank your interviewee.

Don't rush off, and try not to schedule additional appointments for yourself on the day of the interview. For a one-hour interview, I always set aside the whole morning or the whole afternoon. Your interviewee may be in an "up" mood or may be feeling particularly emotional after sharing and trusting you with private and sometimes long-forgotten memories, so it's a good idea to gently bring your interviewee back to the present by staying for a cup of tea and a chat about everyday things.

If you're continuing the interviews, confirm a time for the next one. As previously mentioned, if your interviewee is elderly, it's a good idea to also later confirm in writing the date and time of the next interview.

Copyright and the Release Form

Many people simply want to share their interview recordings with other family members, but others may also wish to later share it in the wider public domain (write a book, set up a website). Regardless of what you intend to do with the recordings, you must gain explicit permission from your interviewee to record the interviews and, if applicable, to make it available for access and use by others. You should therefore always ensure that your interviewee signs a general release form that clearly states his or her permission to use the recordings and ensure that the form also states any conditions that the interviewee wishes to place upon that permission.

Inform your interviewee that he or she also has the right to review and edit transcripts of the interview and to seal sensitive portions of the interview for specific periods of time. Agree also who will hold the master copy of the interviews and whether the interviewee specifically wishes anyone else to receive a copy. This can all be included on the form if required.

A basic example of a release form is included in the Resources section of this book, and you can adapt this to suit your own requirements and those of your interviewee. Have your interviewee sign two copies of the release form. Keep one copy with the original recordings, and leave one copy with your interviewee for his or her own records.

Copyright, as it relates to oral history recordings, may vary according to the laws of the country in which you live. So if you wish to use your family history interviews in the wider public domain, you should seek legal advice and find out what your obligations are.

What to Do with the Completed Recordings

Ensure that files of all interview recordings are clearly identified. Original recordings should be named on their original media and then moved to a safe, secure digital archive location, such as a high-quality external drive.

Make an additional backup copy of each original recording and store it in a safe place.

Copies of these backup files should be made for editing, noise reduction, or other enhancing work. Do not use the originals for editing.

When you have completed your interviews you may like to write a summary of each one briefly listing the main theme, topics, and stories discussed. This can be helpful if you intend to develop your interviews further into another format, such as a written transcript or book, a set of CDs or recordings in another medium, a family history website, a video, or even a scrapbook. You can supplement this rich tapestry of stories by including photos, letters, and other mementos in whatever final compilation you choose.

Remember to provide your interviewee with a copy of the recordings in a generally accessible format, such as CD, together with a copy of any other products you have developed from the interviews. Also include a handwritten note of thanks.

Easy software packages, such as Express Scribe, are available for transcribing your digital recordings directly from portable recorders. Compatible foot pedals with a USB connection for your computer are also available for hands-free transcription playback.

Chapter 5

Tips for the Interviewee

Before you share your family story, talk to friends or relatives about old times. Ask them what they might like to know about you.

Be yourself. It's your story, and it should reflect the way you really are. Use your own words and use simple language.

Relax. Don't worry about fumbling some of the questions or "doing it right." You'll get the hang of it as you go along, and your interviewer will also feel at ease if the atmosphere lacks a little "formality."

Be honest. Tell your story as you remember it. Don't be swayed by other people's version of the same event and don't be tempted to embellish the truth.

Leave it out. If you are reluctant to tell the full details of some experience, don't feel you have to tell all. Your interviewer will respect your desire not to discuss certain subjects or events.

Be personal. Recall the way you felt about things, and don't be afraid of showing your emotions. Memories can be emotional, and even the most pleasant ones can be exhausting to re-live, but often emotions add the colour to your story; your interviewer will understand and respect that.

Stop the recording. If, for any reason, you would like to stop the recording at any stage during the interview, use a pre-arranged signal to your interviewer like holding up your hand, or simply just say, "Please stop the recording."

Silence is okay. Don't be afraid of periods of silence during the interview. You may need to think a little longer about certain questions, and your interviewer will also understand that.

Use humour. Don't be afraid to laugh at some of the mistakes you have made in your life. This is your chance to remember the good times and laugh again!

Provide detail. Recall the environment of your stories—the weather, sounds, smells, tastes, touch, colours, names, descriptions, and timing; everything you can remember adds to the enjoyment of your story.

Use props. Let your interviewer know beforehand if you have any family charts, letters, diaries, photographs, or other treasured items that you might like to use to help your memories to come flooding back. Your interviewer will know how to include details of these in the recording.

Provide context. Fix your stories in time by relating them to significant events in the wider world. For example, political events, sporting events, disasters, and famous personalities can provide great context for an event in remembering other details.

Provide a message. Share your wisdom. Consider the implication of the fact that your stories may be read or heard by your descendants in one hundred or two hundred years' time! So don't be afraid to tell them what mistakes you made and what you've learnt about life.

Chapter 6

How to Ask Questions

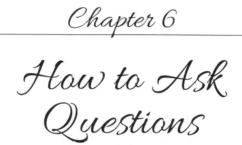

Interview Introduction

Don't forget to turn the recorder on! Then begin each new interview recording with an introduction that identifies yourself, your interviewee, and the date of the interview. Adapt the examples below as appropriate for your own interviews.

First Interview: Introduction Example

This is an interview with Mr. John Brown talking with Sally Smith about the Brown family history. Today is

Monday the twenty-second of March, 2013, and we're recording this at Mr. Brown's home at 25 Jones Street, Smithville, Victoria.

Second and Subsequent Interviews: Introduction Example

We're continuing the interview with Mr. John Brown talking with Sally Smith about the Brown family history. Today is Wednesday the twenty-fourth of March, 2013.

If you're using an old **analogue** cassette recorder, remember to identify the position of each recording in the interview sequence. Use the *First Interview Introduction Example* above as a guide and also identify your cassette by saying, "This is cassette one, side A." Identify the second side of your cassette by simply saying, "This is cassette one, side B." There's no need to record another full introduction on side B, but you can if you like. If you use more than one cassette for an interview – and at the beginning of subsequent interviews – use the *Second Introduction Example* above as a guide and remember to identify each side of each cassette you use.

If you're recording in a **digital** format, for your first interview, use the *First Introduction Example* above as a guide. For subsequent interviews, use the *Second Introduction Example* above as a guide. If necessary, you can manipulate the positioning of your introductions in the final recordings (by using Audacity or other audio editing software) when you transfer them to CD or to whatever final media format you choose to use for your project, so that they fit and flow smoothly in that format.

A read/write CD holds approximately seventy minutes' recording time. If you intend to transfer your final recordings to CD, try to time your line of questioning about a particular topic to end at around the sixty-minute mark. This provides a bit of flexibility for your interviewee to finish talking about a particular subject on one CD rather than having to continue the story on another.

Interview Technique

It is up to you to get the best recording you can by guiding the narrator in telling his or her story. Much of the skill involved in interviewing is listening and taking in what your interviewee is saying, whilst at the same time thinking ahead about where you could take a particular line of questioning or what you might ask next. This can be quite daunting for a novice interviewer, so just remember to be yourself; if you're relaxed, then your interviewee will be relaxed as well. Don't worry about fumbling some of the questions or "doing it right." You'll get the hang of it as you go along, and your interviewee will feel more at ease if the atmosphere lacks a little formality. If you do feel a bit overwhelmed about being responsible for conducting the whole interview, perhaps—with the agreement of your interviewee—you could enlist the help of a family member or friend to monitor the recording whilst you ask the questions.

Before you start, take a look at the question list in chapter 7, develop an overall plan of the topics you want to cover, and group your preferred questions in a logical way. During the interviews, after gathering some basic facts, you'll focus on eliciting stories, feelings, and descriptions about events and experiences by using open-ended questions of your own that encourage personal observations rather than *yes* or *no* answers.

In the "settling down" phase at the beginning of the first interview, ask easy questions like the brief, biographical questions listed at the start of chapter 7. Then ask your first substantial question, which will get your interviewee "going" on the subject. If you prepare a short summary after each interview listing the main theme, topics, and stories discussed, you can start subsequent interviews by briefly recapping the previous conversation, which will provide a great ice-breaker.

Listen carefully to what your interviewee is saying so that you can follow up on leads into other stories. Don't get distracted or become inattentive; if you lose the thread of the conversation it can be a little difficult to get back on track. However, also keep in mind as you go along that the story can take as many twists and turns as you like; so don't be afraid to let your interviewee wander down paths you hadn't originally intended.

When this happens and you feel ready to draw a narrative to a close, find an appropriate place in the story to gently bring your interviewee back to your original line of questioning.

If, after you have finished with a particular topic, you think of another question you would like to ask, make a note of it and ask it at the end of the interview. It doesn't matter if some parts of the story are not in perfect sequence. You can simply leave them where they are to form part of the interesting progress of the interview, or you can later cut and paste them into a more sequential place in the recording when you transfer it to a CD or other format that allows it to be edited first.

Remember that it can be confusing for anyone, particularly an elderly person, to be asked to jump back and forth in their minds to different parts of their lives. Also remember that people don't always speak in complete sentences at the best of times—they repeat themselves and leave things out, and they talk in circles and tell fragments of the same story out of chronological sequence. Our memory plays tricks on us, and sometimes it's hard to find the right word for our thoughts, especially with someone listening and recording what we are saying—even if you are family. So be patient and allow the memories to flow from one time period to another. Don't worry if this sounds a bit daunting. You will quickly get the hang of it because you have a personal interest in your interviewee and their story.

You can use, as a memory jogger, a brief "cheat sheet" of key words using the questions listed in chapter 7 as a guide, but if you prefer to have a printed list of questions in front of you, don't distract your interviewee or spoil the recording by rustling papers whilst they are talking. I use a two-ring binder into which I insert printed pages of my questions in separate plastic sleeves. They are quieter to turn, and I make reminder notes on a separate notepad as I go along.

Phrase your questions in your own words, and use plain language, not jargon. Be polite and attentive throughout the interview, and wait until your interviewee has completely finished answering a question before asking a new one.

Ask questions one at a time in simple sentences. Questions that have more than one part can be confusing, and your interviewee will likely only answer the last part.

Encourage the interviewee to give his or her own impressions and opinions; don't dominate the conversation or correct your interviewee. Don't state your personal opinion, as your interviewee may feel uncomfortable not agreeing with you. For example, you might ask, "How did you feel when …?"; "How did you feel about …?"; "What was your concern about …?"; or "Why was that?"

Some questions may overlap others that you have already raised. Ask these additional questions in a way that makes it clear you have touched on this subject previously but are requesting more information on the topic. For example, at the beginning of the interview, when recording details about a spouse, your interviewee may have, at the same time, spoken about their relationship, where they met, their wedding day, and the like. So when you ask questions on this topic later in the interview you might say, for example, "I know we briefly covered … but now I'd like to ask you about … relating to …."

Ask questions that encourage your interviewee to give details and to tell stories or to give specific examples. If your interviewee makes a general statement or gives a one-word answer, say that you'd like to know more. For example, you might ask, "Why?"; "How?"; or "What?" You might use phrases like "Tell me about …"; "What do you remember about …?"; "What do you mean by …?"| "Where did that take place?"; "Who else was with you when …?"; or "What else can you tell me about …?"

Ask your interviewee to clarify the spelling of names or places, and ask for definitions and explanations of unusual words that may have a critical meaning for the interview. This clarification can be particularly useful if the interview is being transcribed.

Encourage your interviewee to reconstruct physical environments. For example, you might ask, "Could you take me on a walk through the house?" Encourage your interviewee to remember routines, smells, tastes, and sounds.

If you ask questions that require a single-word reply (such as a date) or a *yes* or *no* answer, the interviewee will often respond with that answer and then stop talking. They will offer no further information, thinking that the question has been answered. You're better off to ask, "Can you tell me more about that?" or other questions beginning with *when, where, why,* or *how.*

Ask questions that encourage your interviewee to provide more details and to tell interesting stories about their passions and values, and what lessons they have learned in life. For example, you might ask, "How did you feel about that?"; "What do you mean by that?"; and "Can you describe that in more detail?"

Many people do not remember dates but can place experiences in their lives in relation to certain events or in chronological sequence. In establishing a date that may have been forgotten, you could ask, "What happened next?"; "How old were you when that happened?"; or "Was that before or after you were married?"

The audio recorder can't record any gestures your interviewee makes when describing something, so, where possible, verbally verify these. For example, if your interviewee gestures with his or her hands apart whilst saying, "The fish was this big," you could verbally verify by asking, "About eighteen inches long?"

If your interviewee becomes emotional during the interview, ask if they would like you to pause the recording. You may want to agree on a pre-arranged signal for this, such as holding up a hand, or agree that they can simply just say, "Please stop the recording." Memories can be emotional, and even the most pleasant ones can be exhausting to re-live. However, emotions are often an important part of the interview and are well worth leaving in the recording if possible.

If your interviewee becomes unwilling to discuss certain subjects or events, respect their wishes, and don't push for answers. You may have to skip those questions and move on to something else or even end a session sooner than planned. However, if you have established that your interviewee is prepared to talk about a sensitive topic, encourage them to keep talking and don't be tempted to give your personal opinion of their response. For example, you might say, "That must have been very difficult for you," and continue with, "How did you feel about …?"

If your interviewee seems to be flagging a little, use verbal encouragement like "How interesting," and they will often tell you more about the topic.

Let your interviewee know when you are moving to a new line of questioning so that they have a clear idea of what is to follow. For example, you could say, "I'd now like to move on to something else and ask you about …"

Take an active part in the dialogue by asking the questions, but don't comment whilst your interviewee is speaking. This is very important, because the recording can be ruined by an interviewer constantly interjecting comments like *uh huh*, *oh really*, and *mmm*. Although these comments can be deleted from a digital recording, it takes time, which is sometimes an extra expense, to do so.

Let your interviewee know that you will communicate interest in what he or she is saying by giving silent responses, such as leaning forward, maintaining eye contact, nodding, smiling, and "silent laughter." This is a very important skill to develop in order to get a clean, uncomplicated recording. If you must laugh out loud, wait until your interviewee has finished speaking so that his or her voice is clearly heard throughout the recording; you can edit out your laughter afterwards if necessary. This point may seem to be a bit finicky, and you may think that by remaining silent during a humorous story will seem impolite or indifferent because of the family nature of your interview. But we're talking here about getting a good recording that future generations of your family can enjoy, so leave it up to them to laugh out loud at your interviewee's stories—they will thank you for doing such a great job of ensuring that they are able to clearly hear every word!

Don't be afraid of periods of silence or a longish pause in the interview. A pause can be part of your interviewee's natural speech pattern or they may be taking a little time to call up memories of events that they may not have thought of in years. When there is a period of silence or a pause, be patient and wait it out; your interviewee may be reflecting on something that you may not have thought to ask about, or they may be preparing to tell you a story that turns out to be one of the most inspiring parts of the interview, so don't rush them!

Your interviewee may need to explain comments. A few examples I have encountered were "Our dog was just like the one we have now, but his back and neck were the same colour as that rug," and, "It stood about this high, a bit smaller than my mother's china cabinet over there, the one with the shield and sword on the wall above it." The latter statement alone led to a couple more interesting stories!

Explain any interruptions before you stop the recording. For example, you could say, "I'll just stop the recording now because ..." Then when you start recording again you could say, "So let's get started again ... You were telling me about ..." This puts your interviewee at ease and avoids confusion for listeners.

Family charts, letters, photographs, and treasured items may help your interviewee to bring memories flooding back, so use props if appropriate. However, for the purposes of the recording, ask your interviewee to explain in context what it is that they are showing you.

At the end of each interview, always ask if there is anything else that the interviewee would like to say.

If you feel that—when the recordings are made available to others— comments made by the interviewee might be construed as defamatory towards another living person, their character, or their reputation, stop the recording and explain this to your interviewee and the reason why. Obtain your interviewee's agreement to leave out that particular part of the story altogether, or encourage your interviewee to continue the interview without the defamatory words. You could begin that part of the interview again and edit out the potentially defamatory section later; or if you're recording in an analogue format, simply rewind the cassette and record over the inappropriate section.

Remember, this is *your* family history venture. So use the above tips to guide you towards what works best for you in developing a comfortable interview method for getting a great recording.

Chapter 7

Questions to Ask

This list of questions will give you an idea of topics that can be explored when recording your family history. It is by no means an exhaustive list. Please include your own personal questions and omit those that do not suit your requirements. It is up to you to ask follow-up questions that will enable you to tease out any interesting stories that may arise from your line of questioning as you progress through each interview.

Early Family Years and Your Relatives

1. What is your full name?
2. What is your maiden name?
3. Do you know why your Christian name was chosen for you?
4. Were you named after a relative or someone famous?
5. Is there a naming tradition in your family?
6. What do you know about your family surname? What is its origin?
7. Has the spelling been changed at some point in the past?
8. Have you ever been known by any other names?
9. Did you have a nickname as you were growing up? What was it?
10. Why did they call you that nickname?
11. Have you had any other nicknames as an adult?
12. What do your family call you now?
13. Where and when were you born?
14. Do you remember any stories that your parents shared with you about your birth?
15. What was your father's full name?
16. Where and when was he born?
17. What is the date and place of his death? Where is he buried?
18. Can you tell me any family anecdotes or stories about your father?
19. What was your mother's full name?
20. Where and when was she born?
21. What is the date and place of her death? Where is she buried?
22. Can you tell me any family anecdotes or stories about your mother?
23. What did your parents do for a living before they were married?

24. How did they meet?
25. What date were your father and mother married?
26. Had your father been married before? What was his former wife's name?
27. Was your mother married before? What was her former husband's name?
28. Can you tell me about your grandparents on your father's side?
29. What were their full names (including maiden name)?
30. Where and when were they born?
31. What are the dates and places of their deaths? Where are they buried?
32. Can you tell me any family anecdotes or stories about your father's parents?
33. Can you tell me about your grandparents on your mother's side?
34. What were their full names (including maiden name)?
35. Where and when were they born?
36. What are the dates and places of their deaths? Where are they buried?
37. Can you tell me any family anecdotes or stories about your mother's parents?
38. Did you know your grandparents very well?
39. Where did they grow up?
40. How did your grandparents meet?
41. Did they live nearby?
42. Did you spend much time with them?
43. Did they have any funny mannerisms?
44. Do you remember any of the stories they used to tell you?
45. Do you remember hearing your grandparents describe their lives? What did they say?
46. Did they keep any records of their daily lives?
47. Do you have any special memories of your grandparents or of times you spent with them?
48. Did your grandparents ever talk to you about your parents growing up?
49. What did they say?
50. Who was the oldest relative you remember as a child? What do you remember about them?
51. Do you have any brothers or sisters?
52. What are their full names (including maiden name)?

53. Where and when were they born?

54. Are they still alive? If yes, where are they living now? Do you see each other often?

55. If no, what were the dates and places of their deaths? Where are they buried?

56. Did they marry? What are the names of their husbands or wives?

57. Were you close to your brothers or sisters as a child?

58. Can you tell me any interesting stories about growing up with your brothers or sisters?

59. Do you have nieces and nephews?

60. What are their full names (including maiden name)?

61. Where and when were they born?

62. Do you keep in touch with any of them? If so, what are they doing now?

63. What was your birth position in the family—eldest, youngest?

64. Were you treated any differently? What were the advantages and disadvantages?

65. Were you brought up by anyone other than your parents?

66. Who was this, and why did this happen?

67. Were you spoilt as a child?

68. Did you have to shoulder more responsibility than your brothers and sisters?

69. Did you feel you were a "black sheep" in your family, or did you feel left out in any way?

70. How did you react to the way your family treated you?

71. Were you encouraged to be independent?

72. Do you feel your views and opinions were valued within the family circle?

73. Do you feel you displayed characteristics that were unique in your family?

74. How did your family members interact with one another generally?

75. Was your home life harmonious, or were there conflicts?

76. Did any particular family members clash with each other?

77. Were any particular family members more easy-going than others?

78. Did anyone have a good sense of humour? Do you have any funny stories about that?

79. Can you describe the personalities of your parents and your siblings?
80. What was discipline like in your family?
81. Who wielded the most authority?
82. Were rules set down about how you were expected to behave?
83. Did you get into trouble? What was the worst thing you did?
84. Were you punished for misbehaving?
85. Do you remember any particular punishment you received?
86. How did you feel about punishment? Did it deter you from misbehaving again?
87. Were you rewarded for good deeds or good behaviour? How were you rewarded?
88. How would you describe your parents?
89. Were they loving and kind?
90. Did they enforce strict discipline in your family?
91. Were they willing to teach you independence?
92. Were they easy-going or pedantic?
93. How would you describe your relationship with your parents?
94. How tall are you?
95. What colour are your eyes?
96. What colour was your hair as a young child and then as an adult?
97. What particular traits do you think you have inherited from your parents?
98. Do you feel that you are like your grandparents in any way?
99. Did one or both of your parents work when you were a child?
100. What were their occupations?
101. Did you ever have to help in any way with your parents' work?
102. How did you help, and did you like doing this?
103. Did two incomes provide your family with a good standard of living?
104. Was it to make ends meet?
105. How did you feel about both parents working?
106. Did you have to forego anything because your parents couldn't afford it?
107. Were you always alone after school?
108. Did you have to do extra chores to help out?
109. Did your friends' parents work?

110. Did you ever feel underprivileged in any way compared with your friends?
111. Did any of your relatives ever help your family out financially?
112. What were your family's living standards like when you were growing up?
113. Did you grow your own food?
114. Did your mother make your clothes?
115. Could your parents afford any luxuries?
116. Did your parents teach you any special skills, such as cooking, sewing, reading, or music?
117. Did your father play football, soccer, or other sports with you?
118. Did you spend time with your parents whilst they taught you other special skills?
119. Tell me about any events you remember that affected your family as a whole.
120. Were there any family feuds, divorces, or scandals that affected your family?
121. Do you remember any particularly happy, funny, sad, or traumatic events that occurred?
122. Were there any accidents, sicknesses, deaths, or funerals that you remember?
123. Did you attend any weddings, births, or christenings that you remember well?
124. Can you remember who was involved in any of these events, when did they take place and did you play a role?
125. Can you tell me about the rituals that were followed on some of these occasions?
126. Was any special food prepared on these occasions?
127. Was special clothing worn?
128. Was special music played, and who played it?
129. How did these family events affect you as a child and as an adult? (See also Religion.)
130. Were you adopted as a child?
131. Do you know the names of your birth parents?
132. Have you met your birth mother or birth father?
133. How did you meet, and did you like them?

134. When did you find out you were adopted, and who told you?
135. How did this make you feel at the time?
136. How have you dealt with this knowledge throughout your life?
137. How do you feel about it now?
138. Do have any other brothers or sisters from your birth parents?
139. Have you met them?
140. Are they still alive?
141. Do you see each other now?
142. Do you have a story, advice, or special feelings you'd like to share about being adopted?
143. When you were growing up, did you have any favourite aunts or uncles?
144. Who were they?
145. Why were they your favourite?
146. Were there any aunts or uncles you did not particularly like? Why not?
147. Do you have any cousins? What are their names?
148. Were you close to them as a child?
149. Can you tell me about some good times you had with your cousins?
150. Do you still keep in contact? Where are they now?
151. Did any other relatives live with your family when you were growing up?
152. Do you know how this arrangement came about?
153. How did you feel about this?
154. Did this benefit you in any way?
155. Is your family or anyone in your family famous or well known?
156. Can you tell me why?
157. Have you benefited from this?
158. How else has it affected you?
159. Was any family member particularly funny or did any family member have any unusual characteristics?
160. Was anyone the black sheep of your family, or did anyone cause a scandal?
161. Do you have any family heirlooms or special treasures passed down to you from your grandparents or other relatives?
162. Can you remember any particular or funny family expressions or sayings?

163. Where did they come from?
164. Can you tell me any family stories or funny anecdotes about any of your relatives?
165. What is your ethnic background?
166. Did any of your family or ancestors emigrate from another country? Where did they come from? When did they emigrate?
167. Was there a specific reason why they left their home country?
168. How and where did they get the money to travel?
169. When your ancestors emigrated, did they do so with other relatives? Who were those relatives?
170. Where did they settle when they arrived in this country?
171. Who received the relatives when they first arrived in this country?
172. What was the name of the ship they arrived on and the port of entry, or how else did they arrive?
173. What occupations did your immigrant ancestors have?
174. Did they belong to any organizations, churches, or other groups?
175. Where did your immigrant ancestors live in their "old" country?
176. Did they bring with them special heirlooms or traditions that have been handed down?
177. Have you any documents, letters, or photographs about these ancestors?
178. Do you still have relatives who live in another country? Who are they, and where do they live? Have you ever been to visit them? What was that experience like?
179. What traditions did your relatives bring with them to this country?
180. Do you or your children still uphold any of those family traditions?
181. Did they pass on ethnic music or food styles to your family?
182. Can you share any family stories about ancestors who emigrated from another country?
183. Who were your best friends when you were growing up?
184. Can you describe your friendship with them?
185. Can you tell me any favourite stories from your childhood?

Your Childhood Family Home

If you lived in several homes during your childhood, you might like to describe them all, but let's start with your favourite or perhaps the one where you lived the longest.

1. Where was your family home when you were growing up?
2. How did your family come to live there?
3. Did other family members live in the same area? Who were they?
4. What are your earliest memories of your home?
5. Was it a house or a flat?
6. What did it look like from outside?
7. Was it single or double storey?
8. Was it made from bricks, weatherboard, or something else?
9. What did the windows look like?
10. Was there a porch or veranda?
11. Was there a driveway?
12. Did you have a garden? Were there front and back gardens?
13. Were there other buildings on the same property?
14. Was there a fence around the garden?
15. Did you have a vegetable garden or fruit trees? What did you grow?
16. Did you sell the produce?

17. Did your garden have climbing trees? Did you have a swing or a cubby house?
18. Were there any animals that shared your garden?
19. If you lived on a farm, what crops were planted?
20. Who did the work?
21. Did your family raise livestock for a living on the farm?
22. Did your family keep any livestock for food, such as meat, milk, or cheese?
23. If you lived in the city, what was your neighbourhood like?
24. Can you describe the neighbouring homes? Did they have fences around them?
25. Were there parks in your area? Did you ever play in them?
26. What were the streets around your home like? Was there much traffic?
27. Did you have neighbours? Did they live close by or far away?
28. Did your neighbours have special customs?
29. Did you ever stay overnight in their homes?
30. Did your families ever provide special support for each other?
31. If you lived in the country, can you describe the countryside surrounding your home?
32. What were the neighbouring homes like?
33. Was there a town close by? How large was it? Did you go there to shop?
34. Did you have friends in the neighbourhood with whom you played?
35. How did you spend your time with those friends?
36. If you lived in the city, did you have to play in the street?
37. If you lived in the country, where did you play with your friends?
38. What games did you play?
39. What type of entertainment was available in your area?
40. What are some things you particularly remember about living in the city?
41. What are some things you particularly remember about living in the country?
42. Can you describe the layout of the rooms in your childhood home?
43. What were they were used for?
44. Were the floors in your home polished or carpeted?

45. Did the windows have curtains or blinds?
46. Were the walls painted or wallpapered? What colour or pattern were they?
47. What pieces of furniture do you remember in your home?
48. Did you have a lounge suite and a dining suite?
49. What was the bedroom furniture like? How were the bedrooms decorated?
50. Were there any special decorative objects on the walls?
51. Do you remember any other pieces of furniture?
52. How was your home heated? Did your home have a fireplace? Was it warm in winter?
53. Did you burn wood or coal? Did you have to help cut the wood?
54. Where did your family get water? Was it plentiful?
55. Did you have to conserve water? How did you do this?
56. Did you have a telephone? What was this like? Were you allowed to use it?
57. Did you always have electricity? If not, what did you use for lighting?
58. How was the house kept clean? Did your family have a vacuum cleaner?
59. Did you have an iron? How was the ironing done?
60. Did your family always have a refrigerator? If not, what did you use instead?
61. When did you get a refrigerator?
62. Did you have a gramophone, a radio, or a television?
63. Were there any other kinds of appliances you can remember in your childhood home?
64. Did your house have a hallway or stairs?
65. What did these look like? Where did they lead to?
66. Was there an attic?
67. What can you tell me about it?
68. What was stored there?
69. Did your home have a cellar? What was this used for?
70. Was the kitchen a focal point in your home where people gathered? Why was that?
71. Did you eat your family meals in the kitchen or a dining room?
72. Where did you eat when you had visitors?

73. What kind of stove was in the kitchen? How did it work?
74. What kinds of utensils were used in the kitchen?
75. What kind of crockery and cutlery were used?
76. Did you have one set of crockery for everyday and another set that was used for visitors?
77. Was the laundry inside the house or outside?
78. Who did the washing in your family?
79. Was there a routine day when this was done?
80. How were the clothes washed?
81. Did you have a washing machine? How did it work?
82. What kinds of soaps were used to wash the clothes?
83. How were the clothes dried?
84. Can you describe the bathroom?
85. Were there a bath and a shower in the bathroom?
86. Was hot water always available?
87. What colour was the bathroom, and what were the fittings like?
88. Was there a toilet in the bathroom?
89. Was the toilet in a separate room in the house or outside the house?
90. Was it septic or flushing?
91. How many bedrooms did your home have?
92. Did you have a room of your own, or did you share it with someone else?
93. What was this experience like? Do you remember any funny stories about this experience? Where in the house was your bedroom located?
94. What were the colours in your bedroom?
95. Did you choose these colours? Why?
96. How was your bedroom furnished?
97. Were there any other rooms in your home?
98. What were they used for?
99. Did your home have a garage?
100. Where was it located on your property?
101. Did your parents own a car? What make was it? Was it stored in the garage?
102. Did you use any other means of transport when you were growing up?

Family Life When You Were Growing Up

1. What is your earliest childhood memory?
2. What do you remember about your family's daily or weekly routine?
3. How were the household tasks done, and who was responsible for them?
4. Who did the laundry? How was it done?
5. Who did the housework? Who washed the dishes? Who did the ironing and mending?
6. Did you have family chores to do when you were a child or as you grew older?
7. What were they?
8. Which chores did you enjoy? Which were your least favourite?
9. Were these done before or after school or at weekends?
10. Did everyone in the family have responsibility for certain chores?
11. Who usually did the shopping in your household?
12. Were there local shops in your neighbourhood?
13. Where did your family usually shop?
14. Do you remember the shopkeepers' names? What kinds of goods did they sell?
15. Were any goods delivered to your home, such as milk, ice, bread, meat, or vegetables?
16. Did you grow or make your own food (vegetables, fruit, poultry, meat, milk, eggs, or bread)?

17. Can you tell me any interesting stories about going shopping when you were a child?
18. Who usually cooked the family's meals?
19. What kinds of food did your family eat?
20. Can you describe a typical week's meals?
21. What do you remember about mealtimes in your household?
22. Did the family eat together at mealtimes?
23. Did you have any favourite foods?
24. Were there any foods that you disliked? Were you made to eat them?
25. What recipes or meals do you remember that you liked the most?
26. Have any recipes been passed down to you from family members?
27. Did you eat any foods that were considered luxuries at the time?
28. Did you learn to cook? Who taught you?
29. Do you ever remember not having enough food to eat because times were hard?
30. Did your mother or father cut your hair, or did a hairdresser cut it?
31. What hair styles did you wear?
32. Can you tell me any interesting stories about your hair cut when you were a child?
33. What were your dresses, suits, hats, shoes, socks, stockings, and underwear like?
34. Were your clothes bought or made for you?
35. Where did you buy your clothes? Did you have many clothes?
36. Did anyone in your family sew, crochet, embroider, or knit?
37. Did anyone teach you these skills? Who was that? What kinds of things did you make?
38. Where did you buy your shoes? Who repaired your shoes?
39. Do you remember any favourite pieces of clothing or favourite shoes you had?
40. Can you tell me any interesting stories about shopping for clothes or shoes?
41. Were you allowed to wear makeup when you were older?
42. What kind of makeup was it?
43. Did you have any pets or favourite farm animals?
44. Do you remember their names?
45. Do you have a favourite story about any of your pets?

46. Did your family own a telephone? Were you allowed to use it?
47. Did you or your family write letters to friends or relatives?
48. Do you remember anything about the postman delivering letters?
49. Did you ever have a pen friend? Do you still keep in touch?
50. What types of transport were used when you were growing up?
51. Did your family own a horse or a buggy?
52. When did your family acquire its first car?
53. What make was it? What colour was it? How much did it cost to buy?
54. Who usually drove the family car?
55. When did you learn to drive? How old were you? Who taught you?
56. Do you have any funny stories about learning to drive?
57. If you didn't own a car, what transport did your family use?
58. Did you ever travel on a train? Where did you go?
59. Did you have any special hobbies or unique talents? What were they?
60. Did you make a career out of these talents? Do you still use them?
61. How would you describe your family's economic circumstances?
62. Were they rich, middle class, poor or working class, or other?
63. What did this mean to you as a child?
64. What kinds of things would you have called "luxuries" at that time?
65. Did you have many luxuries?
66. Were you given pocket money on a regular basis?
67. How did you have to earn this money?
68. Did you usually spend it or save it?
69. Did your family celebrate Christmas?
70. Did your family celebrate any special traditions at Christmas?
71. Did you always have a Christmas tree? Where did you get it, and how was it decorated?
72. Did your family decorate your house at Christmas?
73. Did you have Christmas stockings? Where did you hang them?
74. Did you receive presents at Christmas? What kinds of presents did you receive?
75. Did your family give each other Christmas presents? What kinds of presents?
76. Did you believe in Santa Claus?
77. How did your family usually spend Christmas Day?
78. Did your family attend church at Christmas?

79. What was Christmas dinner like at your house?
80. Was any special food prepared by your family at Christmas?
81. Did any relatives visit your family on Christmas Day?
82. What was the weather usually like in your neighbourhood at Christmas?
83. Did the weather pose any special problems at Christmas?
84. Did the weather dictate how you spent Christmas Day?
85. What kinds of clothing did you wear at Christmas?
86. How did you feel about Christmas when you were growing up?
87. Does Christmas still evoke those feelings?
88. Did you celebrate the Christmas season at school in any way?
89. Do you have any special memories of your family times at Christmas?
90. Did your family observe Easter?
91. Did your family celebrate any special traditions at Easter time?
92. Was any special food prepared? Were you given Easter eggs?
93. Did your family attend church or any other special celebrations at Easter?
94. Did Easter evoke any special feelings in you? Does Easter time still evoke those feelings?
95. Do you have any special memories of your family times at Easter?
96. How was your birthday celebrated? Did you have a birthday cake?
97. Did you receive presents for your birthday?
98. Was there one present in particular that you remember as the best?
99. Did you have birthday parties? Who came to them? Did you play games?
100. Do you have any special memories of your birthdays?
101. How do you like to celebrate your birthday now?
102. How did your family usually spend the weekends?
103. Was Sunday a special day in your family?
104. Did your family attend church on Sundays? Where did you go?
105. Did you attend Sunday school or church picnics? What are your memories of these?
106. Did the midday dinner have a special place in your family on Sundays?
107. Was there an important annual event in your family's calendar? Did you regularly attend a Show Day? Did your family celebrate any special holidays or memorial days?

108. What special memories do you have of these celebrations?
109. Did you have a family doctor? Did the doctor usually do house calls?
110. Did you ever go to his surgery? What was his surgery like?
111. What kinds of remedies did the doctor use for ailments?
112. Do you remember any emergencies when the doctor was called to your house?
113. Do you have any childhood memories of going to the doctor?
114. Did you have a family dentist? What was his surgery like?
115. What kinds of dental work did you have done?
116. Did going to the dentist frighten you? Why?
117. Do you have any special memories of going to the dentist?
118. How do you feel about going to the dentist now?
119. Were you given any special treatment by your family following a visit to the dentist, doctor, optometrist, or other medical practitioner?
120. Did you wear glasses? Can you remember how you discovered that you needed glasses?
121. Can you describe your visits to the optometrist?
122. What was your first pair of glasses like?
123. How did you feel amongst your peers, wearing glasses?
124. Were you teased by other children because you wore glasses?
125. Did you suffer any childhood illnesses? What were they? How were they treated?
126. Did you have any accidents during your childhood? What happened?
127. Did you spend any time in hospital? What are your memories of that experience?
128. Did anyone from your family stay with you in the hospital?
129. If not, how did you cope alone away from your family?
130. Have any illnesses persisted throughout your life? How have you coped with this?
131. Do you have any health problems that are considered hereditary? What are they?
132. Are you allergic to any drugs? What are they?
133. Do you remember what major events were going on in the world when you were a child?
134. Did any of these events impact on your family and family life? How?
135. Did this make a significant difference in your family life?

136. How did these changes make you feel?
137. How old were you then?
138. Who were your childhood heroes?
139. What did you want to be when you grew up? What inspired you towards this dream?
140. Have you followed or accomplished your dream?
141. Did your dream change over time? How?
142. Were there any particularly important people in your life when you were a child?
143. What made them special to you?
144. How did they influence you?
145. Do you remember any fads from your youth, such as popular hairstyles, clothes, or music?
146. What were your favourite songs as a child?
147. What were your favourite books as a child?
148. What was your favourite music as a child?
149. As a child, did you have a favourite movie or stage actor or singer?
150. Can you describe a perfect family day when you were young?

Your Childhood Family Pastimes

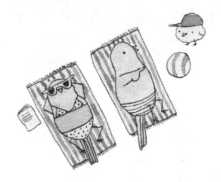

1. Did your family own a wireless or radio or a television set when you were a child?
2. What were the main programs you listened to or watched?
3. Did the whole family listen to or watch these programs together?
4. Did you watch or listen to programs on other people's sets?
5. What did the radio, wireless, or television set look like?
6. What was the reception or station availability like?
7. What shows did you enjoy the most?
8. Did your family own a gramophone, record player, or stereo set?
9. What records did you own?
10. Who were your favourite singers at that time?
11. What were your favourite songs and music?
12. What did the gramophone, record player, or stereo set look like?
13. Did you have books in your home when you were a child?
14. Can you remember some of them?
15. Did someone regularly read to you?
16. Were you encouraged to read as a child?
17. What kind of books did you like to read?
18. What were your favourite books? Who were your favourite authors?
19. Did you belong to a library, or were books bought for you?

20. Do you remember having a favourite nursery rhyme or bedtime story? What was that story?
21. Were newspapers or magazines read in your home? Which ones?
22. Did your family own a set of encyclopaedias?
23. What type of books do you like to read now?
24. Who are your favourite authors?
25. Did you go to the movies, the live theatre, or the drive-in theatre as a child?
26. Who did you go with? Do you remember how much it cost?
27. Can you describe the theatres that you went to?
28. What kinds of shows did you see?
29. What were your favourite shows, films, or actors at that time?
30. What special memories do these times evoke?
31. Did music play a part in your family life?
32. Did you learn to play an instrument? What instrument did you play?
33. Did you have music lessons?
34. Did you play in concerts?
35. Who was your teacher?
36. What were your favourite toys, and what were they like?
37. What were your favourite games and pastimes? (Examples: board games, colouring, comics, annuals, dolls, trains, rocking horse, Meccano set, tea set, skipping rope, tree house, stamp collecting, swimming, cricket, pushbikes, jacks, marbles, football, riding, soccer, rugby, other.)
38. Can you describe how you played them?
39. Did you play make-believe games by yourself or with friends?
40. Can you remember some of these?
41. Were you taken on regular outings as a child? Where did you go?
42. Did you often visit relatives or friends?
43. Did you participate in any sporting activities or watch as a spectator?
44. Did you go on picnics to a beach or swimming spots?
45. Did you attend church activities with your family?
46. Were you taken to the circus or amusement parks?
47. Do you have fond memories of any particular outings as a child?
48. How did you spend your holidays during your childhood?
49. Did you go away on holidays?

50. Where did you go? Who went with you? How did you get there?
51. What special memories do you have about those holidays?
52. Did you live in a cool or cold climate?
53. Did it snow where you lived during the winter months?
54. What was the weather like generally in winter?
55. Did you experience any extreme weather conditions like blizzards?
56. What were these experiences like?
57. Did your family have special winter pastimes?
58. Did you ski or skate? Where did you do this?
59. What did your neighbourhood look like in winter?
60. How did your family spend the winter evenings?
61. Can you remember special places you went in wintertime?
62. What kinds of clothes did you wear in the winter?
63. How did you get to school in winter?
64. What memories do you have of school in winter?
65. Do you remember any particular dangers you were aware of in winter?
66. Did you have special chores you had to do in winter?
67. Did you eat particular foods during winter? How were they prepared?
68. Were any changes made to the inside or outside of your home for the winter months?
69. Does wintertime evoke any special memories for you now?
70. Did you live in a warm or hot climate?
71. Was it near the beach, in the city, or in the country?
72. What was the weather like generally in summer?
73. Did you experience any extreme weather conditions like heat waves or fires?
74. What were these experiences like?
75. Did your family have special summer pastimes?
76. How did you stay cool in summer?
77. What did your neighbourhood look like in summer?
78. Can you remember any special places you went in summer?
79. What clothes did you wear in the summer?
80. How did you get to school in summer?
81. What memories do you have of school in summer?
82. Do you remember any particular dangers you were aware of in summer?

83. Did you have special chores you had to do in the summer?
84. Did you eat any particular foods during summer? How were they prepared?
85. How did your family spend the summer evenings?
86. Were any changes made to the inside or outside of your home for the summer months?
87. Does summertime evoke any special memories for you now?

Your Primary School Years

1. Where did you go to primary school? Where was it located? What years did you attend?
2. Was it a mixed school or single-gender school?
3. Did your parents pay for you to attend this school?
4. Can you describe the school from the outside?
5. Can you describe the inside of the school?
6. What did the classrooms look like?
7. Were they hot in summer or cold in winter?
8. Were there many pupils in the school? How large were your classes?
9. How did you get to and from school?
10. If you walked to school, was this a hardship in winter or in summer?
11. How far was it to school? How long did it take you?
12. Did you travel to and from school alone or with friends or family?
13. What time did primary school start and finish?
14. What time did you leave home in the morning?
15. What time did you get home in the afternoon?
16. What did you wear to school? What kind of school bag did you carry?
17. Do you remember your first day at primary school?
18. Was it a happy day for you?
19. Did you meet one special person that day?
20. Did you mix with the other children easily that day?
21. Did any of your siblings attend the same primary school?
22. Did they look after you on your first day there?
23. Did you have many friends at primary school?

24. Did you have a best friend then?
25. Have you remained friends with anyone from your primary school days?
26. Have you been to any primary school reunions?
27. How do your fellow classmates from school remember you best?
28. Do you have any photos from your primary school days?
29. What were your daily routines when you went to primary school?
30. Were there any religious or other daily rituals you performed at school?
31. What did you usually do at morning tea time?
32. What did you usually do at lunch time?
33. What kind of food did you take to school?
34. How did these routines differ in winter and summer?
35. Did you go straight home after school?
36. Did you attend extracurricular activities? What were they?
37. Did you have chores to do before and after school?
38. What did you usually do when you arrived home?
39. Was there a chore you really hated doing then?
40. Did you have homework each night?
41. What subjects were you taught at primary school?
42. What was your favourite subject? Why?
43. What subject did you like the least? Why?
44. What subject was the easiest for you? Why?
45. What subject was the hardest for you? Why?
46. What teaching methods were used?
47. What did you write with?
48. Did you use exercise books and textbooks? Who supplied those?
49. Do you remember any of your teachers from primary school?
50. Who was your favourite teacher?
51. Why was he or she special to you?
52. Were there any teachers who you did not get along with? Why was that?
53. Did you participate in sport in primary school?
54. What teams did you play with?
55. Did you receive recognition for achievements in sport at primary school?

56. Did you continue to play that sport throughout your life?
57. What other school activities did you participate in at primary school?
58. Did you receive recognition for any achievements in those school activities?
59. What were you given as a prize?
60. Did you like primary school?
61. Were you a conscientious student, or did you misbehave?
62. What kinds of activities were punished at primary school?
63. How were you disciplined at primary school (detentions, caning, cleaning up playground, line writing, or other)?
64. Were you ever rewarded for good behaviour or good work?
65. Do you remember any favourite songs, poems, or stories you learnt at primary school?
66. What were they? Why did you particularly like them?
67. Were there children at primary school who were different or disadvantaged in any way?
68. What kinds of special treatment were they given?
69. Were you treated differently at school for any reason? How did you feel about this?
70. Do you recall particularly memorable things about your primary school days?
71. Did you go on excursions?
72. If you went to a mixed-gender school, did the boys tease the girls?
73. Was there a class or school bully?
74. Did anyone have any memorable nicknames?
75. Was there a class clown?
76. Were there special ways you celebrated world, community, or calendar events at primary school (Christmas, Easter, Olympic Games, visit of royalty or other dignitaries to your country, local region celebrations, the advent of certain inventions, discoveries, and the like)?
77. Were you at primary school during a war?
78. How did this event affect your daily routine at school?
79. What special memories do you have of this event?
80. How did the war affect your family's daily routine?
81. What was going on in your family during your primary school years?
82. What was your father's or mother's job at this time?

83. Where did you live, and who lived with you then?
84. Do you recall any particular celebrations or memorable events that took place within your family during this time?
85. Can you tell me anything else that you particularly remember about your primary school years?
86. Did you enjoy your primary school years?
87. If you could have changed anything about this time, what would it have been?

Your High School Years

1. Did you attend high school?
2. Which high school did you attend? Where was it located? What years did you attend?
3. Was it a mixed school or a single-gender school?
4. Did your parents pay for you to attend this school?
5. Can you describe the school from the outside?
6. Can you describe the inside of the school?
7. What did the classrooms look like? Were they hot in summer or cold in winter?
8. Were there many pupils in the school? How large were the classes?
9. How did you get to and from high school?
10. If you walked to school, was this a hardship in winter or in summer?
11. How far was it to school? How long did it take you?
12. Did you travel to and from school alone or with friends or family?
13. What time did high school start and finish?
14. What time did you leave home in the morning?
15. What time did you get home in the afternoon?
16. What did you wear to school? What kind of school bag did you carry?
17. Do you remember your first day at high school? Was it a happy day for you?
18. Did you meet one special person that day?
19. Did you mix with the other students easily that day?

20. Did any of your siblings attend the same high school?
21. Did they look after you on your first day there?
22. Did you make friends easily at high school?
23. Did you have many friends there?
24. Did you have a best friend at then?
25. What was your social group like at high school?
26. Do you still keep in touch with any high school friends?
27. Have you been to any high school reunions?
28. How do your fellow classmates from high school remember you best?
29. Do you have any photos from your high school days?
30. What were your daily routines when you went to high school?
31. Were there any religious or other rituals you performed at school each day?
32. What did you usually do at morning tea time?
33. What did you usually do at lunch time?
34. What kind of food did you take to school?
35. How did these routines differ in winter and summer?
36. Did you go straight home after school?
37. Did you attend extracurricular activities? What were they?
38. What did you usually do when you arrived home?
39. Did you have other chores to do before and after school? What were they?
40. Is there a chore you really hated doing then? Why?
41. Did you have homework each night?
42. Did you work at a job in the afternoons or weekends whilst you were at high school?
43. Where did you work? What did you do there? How much did it pay?
44. Did you work to make yours or your family's circumstances easier?
45. What did you spend your earnings on?
46. What subjects were you taught at high school?
47. Which subject did you like the most? Why?
48. Which subject did you like the least? Why?
49. What subject was the easiest for you? Why?
50. What teaching methods were used? What did you write with?
51. Did you have exercise books and textbooks? Who supplied those?
52. Do you remember any of your teachers from high school?

53. Did you have a favourite teacher?
54. Why was he or she special to you?
55. Were there any teachers who you did not get along with? Why was that?
56. Did you participate in sport in high school?
57. What teams did you play with?
58. Did you receive recognition for achievements in sport at high school?
59. Did you represent your high school in sport?
60. Did you continue to play that sport throughout your life?
61. What other school activities did you participate in at high school?
62. Did you receive recognition for any achievements in those school activities?
63. What were you given as a prize?
64. Did you like high school?
65. Were you a conscientious student there, or did you misbehave?
66. What kinds of activities were punished?
67. How were you disciplined?
68. Were you ever rewarded for good behaviour or good work?
69. Were you a prefect, or did you hold any other type of student office?
70. Do you remember any favourite songs, poems, or stories you learnt at high school?
71. What were they? Why did you particularly like them?
72. Were there any students at your high school who were different or disadvantaged?
73. What kinds of special treatment were they given?
74. Were you treated differently at school for any reason?
75. How did you feel about this?
76. Do you recall particularly memorable things about your high school days?
77. Did you go on excursions, camps, or trips away for other reasons?
78. Was there a class or school bully?
79. Did anyone have any memorable nicknames?
80. Was there a class clown?
81. When did you graduate from high school?
82. Did you attend a graduation ceremony or dance?

83. What do you remember about this event? What did you wear? Who was your partner?

84. Does this memory evoke any special feelings for you now?

85. Were there special ways you celebrated world, community, or calendar events at high school (Christmas, Easter, Olympic Games, visit of royalty or other dignitaries to your country, local region celebrations, the advent of certain inventions, discoveries, and the like)?

86. Were you at high school during a war?

87. How did this event affect your daily routine at school?

88. What special memories do you have of this event?

89. How did the war affect your family's daily routine?

90. What was going on in your family during your high school years?

91. What was your father's or mother's job at this time?

92. Where did you live, and who lived with you then?

93. Do you recall any particular celebrations or memorable events taking place in your family during this time?

94. Can you tell me anything else you particularly remember about your high school years?

95. Did you enjoy your high school years?

96. If you could have changed one thing about this time, what would it have been?

Your Further Education

1.   Did you attend any school or further training after high school?
2.   What did you study? Where did you study?
3.   Did you complete your study? What qualifications did you achieve?
4.   Did you excel in any area of this study?
5.   How was your tuition paid for?
6.   How much did it cost?
7.   Did your parents pay your fees, or did you have to find a job to support yourself?
8.   Did you receive a scholarship, or did you have to leave home to pursue your tertiary education?
9.   Did you live on campus? What are your memories of campus life generally?
10. What were the campus buildings like?
11. Did you live elsewhere? What memories do you have about that?
12. Did you enjoy this time?
13. Were you involved in any extracurricular activities at your place of study?
14. Were you involved in any political protests or causes on campus?
15. Did you participate in sporting, musical, or dramatic societies on campus?
16. Do you remember your lecturers or teachers during this time?

17. Was there any particular person who inspired you during your tertiary study?
18. Did you undertake on-the-job study, such as an apprenticeship or internship?
19. Did your employers make this easy or difficult for you to do?
20. Where did you work during this time?
21. How did you organise your study and work commitments?
22. How did you decide on a career?
23. Did you pursue a lifelong career in your area of study?
24. Was it a trade, or was it a profession?
25. Did this path provide you with financial stability for the rest of your life?
26. Were you satisfied with your choice of study?
27. What sort of social life did you have during this time?
28. Who were your friends at the time?
29. Do you still keep in contact with any friends you made at this time?
30. Was it difficult for you to be allowed to undertake tertiary study? Why was this?
31. How did you overcome this difficulty?
32. Would you say that you became successful in your field anyway?
33. Did you have the opportunity to undertake tertiary study but rejected it?
34. Was the decision beyond your control?
35. What circumstances prevented you from pursuing further education?
36. Do you now regret this decision?
37. How would your life would have been different had you undertaken tertiary study?
38. Did your parents support your decision to pursue tertiary study?
39. Did they have high expectations of you regarding study and your career?
40. Do you feel that you fulfilled those expectations?
41. Did you try to fulfil their expectations, or were you driven by your own?
42. What advice would you give today's youth about the importance of education?

Your Adult Life and Career

1. When did you leave your parents' home?
2. Why did you leave?
3. What was your first paid employment after you left home or graduated?
4. How did you apply for this? Do you remember the interview?
5. What were the wages?
6. Did you mix well with your co-workers and boss?
7. What skills did you need or acquire for this employment?
8. How long did you keep this position? Why did you leave?
9. Do you work now?
10. If yes, how did you get into this line of work?
11. Do you like what you do for a living?
12. Is this what you thought you would be when you grew up?
13. If no, what did you want to be when you grew up?
14. Can you describe any other employment you have worked at?
15. How did you apply for these positions?
16. Do you remember the interviews? What were the wages?
17. What skills did you need or acquire for these?
18. How long did you keep these positions? Why did you leave?
19. Was it difficult for you to find employment throughout your life?

20. Do you feel that you received lucky breaks?
21. Which of the jobs you have done have you found the most enjoyable? Why?
22. Were you ever employed somewhere that you did not enjoy? Why not?
23. Did you continue your career after your marriage?
24. Did you stay at home and raise a family after you were married?
25. Did you enjoy this?
26. What did you like most about that time?
27. Did you pursue a career before you were married or before you had a family?
28. Do you regret not pursuing a career outside the home?
29. Were you able to do paid work at home? What did you do?
30. What aspects of your career or working life would you like to have done differently?
31. Did your career choice ever allow you to become prominent, famous, or well known?
32. How did this happen? When did this happen?
33. Did this lead to other career opportunities?
34. Did you ever encounter discrimination in your working career?
35. How did you deal with this?
36. Did it adversely affect your career prospects?
37. Did it enhance your career prospects?
38. Have you ever been unemployed?
39. What were the circumstances that led to this?
40. How did this situation make you feel?
41. Did your family suffer financial or other hardship during the time you were unemployed?
42. How did you overcome this?
43. Have you ever been self-employed?
44. Did you prefer to be self-employed rather than work for a boss?
45. How did you set up your business?
46. What line of work were you in?
47. What sort of employer would you describe yourself as?
48. Were/are you successful in this business?
49. Have you ever experienced difficult times whilst running your own business?

50. What advice would you give to young entrepreneurs today?
51. Do you plan on retiring?
52. If so, when will you retire, and how do you feel about it?
53. What do you plan to do in your retirement?
54. Do you have any stories you'd like to tell about your working life?

Love and Marriage

1. What was your first serious relationship?
2. Have you ever been married? (Or ask the question "Have you ever had a special love relationship?" If this question is asked, adjust the following questions as appropriate.)
3. What is your husband's/wife's name (and maiden name)?
4. Where and when was he/she born?
5. What is the date and place of his/her death? Where is he/she buried?
6. Was your husband/wife married before?
7. What was the name of his/her previous spouse?
8. When and where did you meet your husband/wife?
9. What did you do the first time you went out together?
10. What do you particularly remember about your courtship?
11. When did you first fall in love?
12. Was it love at first sight?
13. How did you know that your husband/wife was Mr./Miss Right?
14. How did you or your spouse propose? Where and when did this happen?
15. Did you have a formal engagement? What did you do for this?
16. Did you have an engagement ring? What was it like? How much did it cost?
17. Did you choose the ring together, or was it a surprise?
18. How long were you engaged before you married?

19. How old were you both when you married?
20. How would you describe your husband/wife?
21. What was the most endearing quality that led you to choose your husband/wife?
22. Where did your spouse's parents live?
23. Did you see them often during your marriage?
24. Do you remember anything about the death of your husband's/wife's parents?
25. What date were you married?
26. Where were you married? What time were you married?
27. What did you wear?
28. What did your husband/wife wear?
29. What was the bridal bouquet like?
30. How many bridesmaids and groomsmen did you have? What did they wear?
31. What were the names of the bridesmaids?
32. What were the names of the groomsmen?
33. What was the name of the best man?
34. What was the name of the matron of honour?
35. What was the weather like on your wedding day?
36. Did you marry in a church? If not, where was the ceremony held?
37. How did you and your husband/wife arrive at the church?
38. Who gave the bride away?
39. Do you remember the actual wedding ceremony?
40. Can you describe your feelings during that time?
41. Where was the wedding reception held?
42. What can you remember about the food at the reception?
43. What can you remember about the music at the reception?
44. What can you remember about any speeches that were given?
45. What can you remember about any wedding gifts you received?
46. Can you remember some of the guests' names who attended your wedding?
47. Did you have wedding photographs taken? Where are the photographs now?
48. Do you have any unusual, funny, or embarrassing recollections about your wedding day?

49. If you could have your wedding day over again, would you do anything differently?
50. Did you have a honeymoon?
51. Where did you go? How long did you stay there?
52. Do you have any special recollections of that time?
53. Did you have any preconceived ideas about marriage?
54. In what ways did your marriage turn out to be different than you had expected?
55. Was your relationship with your spouse easy, or were there significant differences?
56. How do you think you complemented each other in the marriage?
57. What were the best times in your marriage and the most difficult times?
58. Did you ever contemplate divorce? If yes, can you tell me about it?
59. Have you been married previously?
60. Would you tell me about your other marriages?
61. What was the name of your previous husband/wife (and maiden name)?
62. Where and when was he/she born?
63. Did your previous marriage(s) end in divorce or death?
64. If death, what is the date and place of your previous husband's/wife's death? Where is he/she buried?
65. If divorced, when did that marriage end? Why?
66. Is there anything interesting you'd like to tell me about your previous husband/wife?
67. *(If appropriate, you can ask questions 2–8 again here.)*
68. Who were your close friends after your marriage?
69. What activities did you enjoy together?
70. Are you still in contact with these friends?
71. What advice would you give to your children or grandchildren about love and marriage?
72. If you have never been married, did you ever propose to anyone ?
73. If no, why was that?
74. If yes, would tell me about the proposal?
75. If you have never been married, did you ever receive a marriage proposal?

76. Did you accept?
77. If yes, why didn't the marriage take place?
78. If no, why didn't you accept?
79. If you have never been married, would you like to have been?
80. Looking back, if you had married, how do you think it might have enriched your life?
81. What lessons did you learn from your relationships and/or marriage(s)?
82. Do you have any favourite stories you would like to share about your husband/wife or about your marriage?

Your First Home After Marriage

1. Where did you live immediately after your marriage?
2. Did you live in rental accommodation?
3. Did you live with relatives?
4. Was it a flat/apartment or a house?
5. How long did you live in that home?
6. Did you purchase your own home?
7. How much did you pay for it?
8. How was it financed?
9. Did you have someone build your home for you, or did you buy one already built?
10. How did you choose the area where you purchased your home?
11. Can you remember anything about the day you moved into your first home together?
12. Can you describe the neighbourhood around your first home?
13. Was it in a rural area or in the city?
14. Did you make friends with other married couples or young families in the neighbourhood?
15. Did you mix socially with these people?
16. Did your children attend school together?
17. Have you remained friends with people you met during this time?
18. What are your earliest memories of your first home?
19. What did it look like from outside?

20. Was your home single or double storey?
21. Was it made from bricks, weatherboard, or something else?
22. What did the windows look like?
23. Was there a veranda or porch?
24. Was there a driveway?
25. What do you remember about the garden at your first home?
26. Were there front and back gardens?
27. Were there sheds or storage areas?
28. Was there a fence around the garden?
29. Did you have a vegetable garden? What did you grow? Did you sell the produce?
30. Did your garden have mature trees?
31. Were there any animals that shared your garden?
32. How many bedrooms did your first home have?
33. Where in the house was the main bedroom located?
34. What were the colours in your bedroom? Did you choose these colours? Why did you choose those colours?
35. How was your bedroom furnished?
36. Can you describe the layout of the other rooms in the house and what they were used for?
37. Were the floors in your home polished or carpeted?
38. Did the windows have curtains or blinds?
39. Were the walls painted or wallpapered? What colour or pattern were they?
40. Did your home have a fireplace? Was this a focal point in your home for family gatherings?
41. What pieces of furniture do you remember in your home?
42. Did you buy new furniture when you moved into your first home?
43. Did you have a lounge suite and a dining suite?
44. What was the bedroom furniture like? How were the bedrooms decorated?
45. Were there any special decorative objects on the walls?
46. What kinds of appliances did you have in your first home?
47. What was the telephone like?
48. What kinds of lighting did you have?

49. Did you have a vacuum cleaner? How else did you keep the house clean?

50. Was there an iron? How was the ironing done?

51. Did you have a gramophone, a radio, or a television?

52. Were there any other kinds of appliances you can remember having in your first home?

53. Did your first home have a hallway or stairs?

54. What did these look like? Where did they lead to?

55. Was there an attic? What was stored there?

56. Was the kitchen a welcoming room where people gathered? Why was that?

57. What was the stove like? How did it work?

58. What kinds of utensils did you use in the kitchen?

59. What kind of crockery and cutlery did you have? Was one set used for visitors?

60. Was there a refrigerator or ice chest? How did these work?

61. Did you have a laundry in your first home?

62. Was it inside the house or outside?

63. Who did the washing?

64. How were the clothes washed? Did you have a washing machine? How did it work?

65. What kinds of soaps were used to wash the clothes?

66. How were the clothes dried?

67. Was there a routine day when this was done?

68. Were there a bath and a shower in the bathroom in your first home?

69. Was hot water always available?

70. What colour was the bathroom, and what were the fittings like?

71. Was there a toilet in the bathroom?

72. Was the toilet in a separate room in the house or outside the house?

73. Did your first home have a garage?

74. Where was it located on your property?

75. Did you own a car? What type was it? Was it stored in the garage?

76. Did you use any other means of transport after your marriage?

77. Is there anything else you would like to say about your first home after marriage?

78. *If never married, ask Questions 1–15 here, in that context.*

Starting a Family

1. Do you have any children?
2. What are their names?
3. Where were they born?
4. Are they still living?
5. What were the dates of their deaths? Where are they buried?
6. Did you foster or adopt any children?
7. What are their names?
8. Where were they born?
9. Are they still living?
10. What were the dates of their deaths? Where are they buried?
11. Can you tell me the story about how you came to adopt or foster these children?
12. How long after you were married did you start a family?
13. Did you both make a conscious decision to have children, or did they just arrive?
14. How old were you and your spouse when your first child was born?
15. How old were you both when your subsequent children were born?
16. Do you remember when you found out you were going to be a parent for the first time? How did it feel?
17. Did each pregnancy progress smoothly?
18. What problems did you or your spouse have in pregnancy?
19. Was each pregnancy similar?

20. Did you or your spouse have long or short labours before each birth?
21. What problems did you or your spouse experience in labour?
22. Was each birth similar?
23. Can you remember the weight of each of your children at birth?
24. Was each of your children healthy at birth?
25. How did you feel when you saw your child/children for the first time?
26. Were there any children who did not survive before or after birth?
27. Can you describe your emotions at that time?
28. Can you tell me how you got through that time?
29. How did you feel when you brought each baby home?
30. Were you confident as a new mother or father?
31. Did you have any help at home at that time?
32. Was the task of rearing a new baby shared between you and your spouse?
33. How did your other children react when a new baby was brought home?
34. How did you choose your children's names?
35. Have they lived up to those names in any unique way?
36. Can you describe what each of your children were like as babies?
37. Can you describe what each of your children were like as young children?
38. Would you have liked a larger family?
39. What prevented you from having more children?
40. What did you find most rewarding about being a parent?
41. What was your proudest moment as a parent?
42. How did you learn to be a parent?
43. How has being a parent changed you?
44. Did you spoil any of your children?
45. Were you a strict or lenient parent?
46. What were the hardest moments you had when your children were growing up?
47. Did you find that you had to treat each of your children differently? If so, why?
48. How did you feel when your eldest child went to school for the first time?
49. Did this become easier as other children started school?

50. What did your children do when they were young that really amazed you?

51. Were there any unusual things that your children did regularly when they were young?

52. What was the funniest thing you can remember that one of your children said or did?

53. What did you find most difficult about raising children?

54. If you had to do it again, would you raise your family differently? How?

55. Did you have dreams for your children? What were they? Did they follow them?

56. Do you remember when your last child left home for good?

57. What advice would you offer your own children today about raising children?

58. Can you tell me any favourite stories about your children?

59. Is there anything else that you would like to say about starting and raising a family?

60. If you had no children, was there a reason for this?

The War Years and the Depression

1. Have you fought in any wars in your lifetime?
2. Are there any significant events that you remember during a war, for example Pearl Harbor?
3. Where were you when your country declared war?
4. How did you find out about war being declared?
5. What was your reaction?
6. Did you understand what was happening?
7. What did you think might happen?
8. Did you or your husband/wife go into military service in a war?
9. How old were you when you enlisted?
10. Which branch of the service did you join? What rank did you achieve?
11. What do you remember about the joining-up procedure?
12. What do you remember about the training?
13. What friends did you make during this time?
14. Were you sent away from your home country on active service during the war? Where were you sent?
15. Can you describe the farewell scenes as you were leaving for active service?
16. What were your duties?
17. Can you recall times during your war experience when you were afraid?
18. Did you have direct contact with the enemy during your war service?

19. Did you have any close shaves with injury or death during your war service?
20. Were you injured in the line of duty? What were the circumstances?
21. Did you perform or witness any acts of heroism during your war service?
22. What were your feelings when peace was declared?
23. Where were you at that time?
24. How did you feel about going home?
25. Can you describe your arrival back home?
26. How did you settle back into normal life after you returned from active service?
27. When you were away did you receive parcels or letters from anyone at home?
28. When you were away, did you go on leave at any time? Where did you go?
29. What is your most vivid memory of your participation in the war?
30. What did you do for leisure and entertainment during the war?
31. What friends did you make during your active service?
32. Do you still keep in touch with these friends?
33. Do you participate in your country's memorial activities?
34. Was any member of your family, or were any friends, a casualty of war?
35. How did you and your family cope with this?
36. If your husband/wife went into service, what did you do whilst he/she was away? Where did you live?
37. How did the war affect your immediate family and environment?
38. Did your war experiences change you in any way?
39. What changes occurred in your life during the war years?
40. If you did not participate in active military service, what jobs were available to you during the war years?
41. How did you or those around you support the country's war effort?
42. What are your strongest memories of your time during the war?
43. What lessons did you learn from your war experience that you would like to pass on to your family?
44. How old were you during the Depression of the 1930s?
45. Did you have work, or were you unemployed during this time?

46. What were your feelings about this?
47. What effect did it have on your attitudes, expectations, and self-esteem?
48. What was your family's situation before the Depression?
49. What was your family's situation during the Depression?
50. Did your father or mother lose his or her job during the Depression, or did he or she work?
51. Do you recall how your family made ends meet during the Depression?
52. Were you in a position to assist anyone else who became unemployed during this time?
53. Do you recall any memorable events in the country during the Depression?
54. What means of entertainment were there during the Depression?
55. What long-term effects of the Depression did you witness on the people around you?
56. How did you see your long-term prospects after the Depression?
57. What did your future hold for you?

Religion

1. What was the religion of your parents and your grandparents?
2. Were you baptized? When and where was this?
3. Do you have your baptismal certificates?
4. Does religion play a part in your life now? If so, what are your religious beliefs right now?
5. Do you believe in God? If so, do you think that this faith has given you confidence to travel through life easily?
6. Do you attend church now? Where do you go?
7. Are you involved in your church's activities?
8. Did your early association with religion affect you or assist you in later life?
9. If you don't attend church, is there any reason?
10. Did religion play a significant part in your family's life? How?
11. Did you attend church regularly with your family?
12. Where did you go to church?
13. Did you have any favourite hymns? Can you remember the words?
14. Did you sing in a church choir?
15. Did your family participate socially in your church community? How? Did you enjoy this?
16. Did you attend Sunday school? Did you enjoy this?
17. Were you awarded any prizes?
18. Can you recall some of the activities that you enjoyed at Sunday school?
19. Can you describe the clothes you wore?
20. Did you say grace or any other thanksgiving prayers at meals?
21. Were you made to say your prayers? Tell me about that.

22. Was Sunday dinner an important ritual in your family?
23. How else did your family spend Sundays?
24. Did your family celebrate any significant religious occasions (weddings, christenings, confirmations, funerals, bar mitzvah, or others)?
25. What you can remember about them?
26. Can you tell me about the rituals followed on these occasions?
27. Was special clothing worn on these occasions?
28. Was special food prepared on these occasions?
29. Was there special music played, and who played it?
30. Can you tell me anything else about these religious occasions?
31. Did you or anyone else in your family pursue a religious vocation?
32. Did you/they join a religious order?
33. How did your family react to this choice?
34. Were you given special religious instruction at school?
35. Can you tell me about this?
36. Is there anything else you'd like to tell me about the part that religion played in your life when you were growing up?
37. Have you ever had a profound spiritual moment that you remember in your life? What happened?
38. Do you believe in an afterlife? Do you believe in reincarnation? Tell me how you feel about these things.

Travel and Other Interests

1. Do you enjoy travelling?
2. Where have you travelled throughout your life?
3. What has been your favourite travel destination?
4. Why was it special?
5. What would you say has been your greatest travel adventure so far?
6. Do you have any special stories about your travels that you would like to record?
7. Do you travel alone, or do you have any constant travelling companions?
8. What sparked your interest in travel?
9. What is your favourite mode of travel?
10. What is the most beautiful place you have visited? What was it like?
11. What else can you tell me about your travels?
12. What organisations do you belong to?
13. What role do you play in these organisations?
14. How do you like to have fun?
15. How do you have fun these days?
16. Do you play a musical instrument?
17. What kind of music do you prefer?
18. Who are your favourite performers?

19. Has your taste in music changed over the years?
20. What other interests and hobbies do you have?
21. How often do you spend time on these interests?
22. Do these interests take you away from home at all? Where?
23. What sparked your interest in these hobbies?
24. What else can you tell me about your interests?
25. Were politics a common topic for discussion, debate, or argument in your family?
26. Who generally started these discussions?
27. Did either or both of your parents have strong political views?
28. Did they take an active interest in a political party?
29. Did their own family backgrounds influence their political choices and interests?
30. Were your political views influenced by your parents or someone else?
31. What are your political views now?
32. Have these views changed over the years?
33. Have you ever taken an active interest in a political party or in local or federal government?
34. What was the extent of this involvement?
35. Has there been any particular political event or issue that you felt strongly about?
36. Why was this?
37. Was there one political personality who stands out in your memory?
38. What is your opinion about today's politicians?

Looking Back and Taking Stock

1. Do you have a philosophy of life?
2. Is there a philosopher, teacher, or writer who best expresses your view of life?
3. What events in your life shaped your philosophy?
4. What are the most important things you have learned about life so far?
5. What was the most valuable thing you learned from your parents?
6. Has your life turned out as you imagined it would?
7. How has it been different than what you'd imagined?
8. What was the happiest moment of your life? What was the saddest?
9. What has been your greatest accomplishment so far?
10. What has been your greatest disappointment, frustration, or failure?
11. Do you have any regrets?
12. What are the top five regrets you have about your life?
13. When have you felt most alone?
14. What is the most important thing in your life right now?
15. Do you have any goals at the moment? What are they?
16. If you now could do anything you wanted to do, what would it be?
17. What are the most important lessons you've learned in life?
18. What were the hardest choices you ever had to make?

19. Do you feel you made the right choices?
20. What other choices would you like to have made?
21. Have you ever had friends who were kindred spirits or soul mates?
22. Who were they? Why did you feel a special bond with them?
23. Which of your friends have you known for the longest period of time?
24. How many years have you been friends?
25. Who are your close friends now?
26. Who are the favourite people in your life now?
27. Who was the most important person in your life? Can you tell me about him or her? What lessons did that person teach you?
28. Has any person changed the course of your life by something he or she said or did? Who were they? What did he or she do? How did it change your life?
29. What do you think will be major world events in the next ten years?
30. What do you have to say about the changes that have taken place during your lifetime (consumer goods, customer service, fashion, transport, communication, technology, medicine, politics, and the like)?
31. What kind of world and society do you think your grandchildren might inherit?
32. Do you believe in life after death?
33. Do you believe you will go to heaven?
34. How has your health been throughout your life?
35. Have you had any major illnesses? What were they?
36. Have you spent any length of time in hospital? What was the reason for this?
37. Have you ever had surgery? If so, why?
38. Is there a history of major illnesses in your family that might be inherited?
39. What is your general health like now?
40. Do you have an illness now? Can you tell me about it?
41. Is this illness terminal? If so, how do you feel about dying?
42. Is there anything you would like to put right before you die?
43. How would you like your family and other people to remember you?
44. Do you have, or know of, any special family heirlooms or memorabilia?
45. What is your favourite colour?

46. What is your favourite food to eat?
47. What is your favourite meal?
48. What is your favourite ice cream flavour?
49. What is your favourite restaurant?
50. What is your favourite drink?
51. What is your favourite fruit?
52. What is your favourite vegetable?
53. What is your favourite tree, plant, or flower?
54. What is your favourite book?
55. Who is your favourite author?
56. What is your favourite holiday destination?
57. What is your favourite sport?
58. What is your favourite animal?
59. What is your favourite time of day?
60. What is your favourite season?
61. What is your favourite card game?
62. What is your favourite possession?
63. What is the nicest piece of clothing you have ever worn?
64. Do you have a favourite piece of clothing now?
65. How have your tastes changed over time?
66. What are the main areas in your life where your taste has changed significantly?
67. Do you drive a car now? If so, what type of car do you drive?
68. When did you learn to drive? Who taught you to drive?
69. What make of car did you learn to drive in?
70. Do you have any funny stories about learning to drive?
71. Do you own a computer?
72. If so, do you enjoy using it? If not, would you like to learn to use one?
73. Do you use the Internet? What do you mainly use it for?
74. What do you think about sophisticated technology now available for everyday tasks?
75. Does it make your life easier and more interesting? How?
76. Does less face-to-face customer service make your life more difficult? How?
77. Are there old-fashioned ways of doing things that you prefer?

78. What is your opinion about the changes in social attitudes in today's world (courtesy, vandalism, censorship, marriage, divorce, language, advertising, convenience food, throwaway household items, families, young people, or other)?

79. What do you think about the mix of ethnic cultures in your country today?

80. Do you enjoy the popularity and wide range of ethnic food and music available nowadays?

81. What advice would you give your grandchildren about choosing a career?

82. What advice would you give them about choosing to marry?

83. What advice would you give them about having children and a career?

84. What advice would you give them about raising children?

85. What advice would you give them about managing money?

86. What sort of person would you say you were as a child?

87. Were you independent and self-confident, or did you lack confidence?

88. Were you anxious about the unknown, or were you a risk taker?

89. Did you become happier or more confident as you grew older?

90. What sort of person would you say you were as a young adult?

91. Were you independent and self-confident, or did you lack confidence?

92. How have you as a person changed throughout your life?

93. Did your values change as you grew older?

94. If you could change something about yourself now, what would it be?

95. What are your general feelings about growing up?

96. Which era did you enjoy the most, the '20s, '30s, '40s, '50s, …?

97. What did you enjoy about these years in particular?

98. Is there anything you miss about the way of life then?

99. Do you remember any favourite belongings you had whilst growing up?

100. What made them so special?

101. Do you still have them?

102. Can you describe any particularly funny or embarrassing moments during your life?

103. What has been the most special experience in your life so far?

104. What were your feelings at the time? Why did you feel that way?

105. Who else shared this experience with you?
106. What has been most unpleasant experience in your life so far?
107. What were your feelings at the time? Why did you feel that way?
108. Who or what helped you to cope with this experience?
109. In hindsight, would you have done anything differently in those circumstances?
110. What would you consider the most important inventions during your lifetime?
111. How is the world different from what it was like when you were a child?
112. Do you remember the first time you saw inventions like a television, a refrigerator, and the like?
113. Do you remember your family discussing world events and politics?
114. What leader of your country have you admired most? Why?
115. Did you ever have strong political views?
116. Did your views on politics change as you grew older?
117. How would you describe your political views now?
118. Would you consider yourself to be creative? If yes, in what way?
119. Have you created anything that others have enjoyed?
120. Are you musical?
121. What instruments have you learnt to play? Do you play now?
122. What is your favourite music style?
123. What is your favourite musical instrument?
124. How would you describe your sense of humour?
125. Have you ever played a memorable practical joke on anyone? What was it?
126. Have you ever been somewhere and remember feeling truly at peace and alive?
127. Where were you? What were you doing?
128. How old were you when you retired?
129. When do you want to retire? What will you do then?
130. Have you ever been a victim of a crime? What happened?
131. Have you ever been in a serious accident? What happened?
132. Has anyone ever saved your life? What happened?
133. Have you survived any natural disasters? What happened?

134. Have you ever met anyone famous? Who was this? How did you meet him or her?
135. Have you won any special awards or prizes as an adult? What were they?
136. Why did you receive these?
137. Were they given to you in a ceremony? Describe this.
138. What activities have you especially enjoyed as an adult?
139. Do you have any hobbies now? If so, what are they?
140. How much time do you spend on them?
141. What do you regularly do for exercise now?
142. What one piece of advice would you like to offer the young people of today?
143. What is the nicest thing your best friend or your family would say about you today?
144. What would you consider to be the major turning point in your life?
145. What was the happiest moment of your life? What was the saddest?
146. Do you believe that there is a lesson to be learnt about life? What lesson have you learnt?
147. If you had your time over again, what would you do differently?
148. How would you like to be remembered?
149. Are there any words of wisdom you'd like to pass along to me now?

Chapter 8
Resources

Websites

http://www.giftofmemories.com and http://www.maryjillbellhouse.com
Oral History Australia http://www.oralhistoryaustralia.org.au/
Oral History NSW http://www.ohaansw.org.au
National Library of Australia http://www.nla.gov.au
State Library of New South Wales, Australia http://www.sl.nsw.gov.au
Australian War Memorial http://www.awm.gov.au
International Oral History Association http://www.iohanet.org
Oral History Association of New Zealand http://www.oralhistory.org.nz
The Oral History Society (UK) http://www.ohs.org.uk
Oral History—British Library http://www.bl.uk/oralhistory
Canadian Oral History Association http://www.canoha.ca
The Oral History Association (USA) http://www.oralhistory.org.nz
Oral history in the digital age http://www.ohda.matrix.msu.edu
Discussion list H-OralHist at http://www.h-net.org/~oralhist/
Australian Copyright Council http://www.copywright.org.au

Express Scribe
http://www.nch.com.au/scribe

Audacity
http://www.audacity.sourceforge.net

Dropbox
http://www.dropbox.com/

Sample Pre-interview Form

(Please do not feel obliged to answer all questions; any information you wish to provide will only be used to assist in preparing questions for the recorded interview.)

Surname _____ Given names _____

Maiden name (if applicable) _____

Address_____ Postcode _____

Telephone number _____ Mobile _____

Email _____

Gender _____ Main occupation _____

Date and place of birth _____

Names of siblings _____

Marital status _____ Date of marriage _____

Name of spouse/partner _____

Occupation of spouse/partner _____

Names of children _____

Mother's name _____

Mother's place of birth and date _____

Father's name _____

Father's place of birth and date _____

Mother's occupation _____

_____

Father's occupation _____

Names of maternal grandparents _____

_____

Names of paternal grandparents _____

_____

Places where you grew up _____

_____

Schools you attended _____

_____

Tertiary education _____

_____

Employment/career _____

_____

Other interests _____

_____

Interesting life events/experiences _____

_____

_____

Sample Release Document

(Adapt to your own requirements, or refer to your legal representative or the oral history association in your state for advice.)

I (print name of person interviewed) _____

authorize (print name of interviewer)

_____

to use, or allow others to use, reproduce, or publish (including electronic publication on the Internet), this interview or part of this interview (including any transcript text created as a result of the interview, other related material provided by the interviewee, and any photographs taken during the interview session) subject to any special conditions listed below (cross out whichever does not apply / add special conditions).

I understand that I will receive a copy of the recording of the interview/s and any transcript or other related material produced from the interview/s.

1. No conditions.

2. Conditions: _____

_____

_____

Signature of person interviewed _____

Address of person interviewed _____

_____

Telephone number of person interviewed_____

Email address of person interviewed_____

Signature of interviewer_____ Date_____